ROAD MAP
THROUGH THE
WILDERNESS

Donald F. Claycomb

WESTBOW
PRESS®
A DIVISION OF THOMAS NELSON
& ZONDERVAN

WestBow Press books may be ordered through booksellers or by contacting:

WestBow Press
A Division of Thomas Nelson & Zondervan
1663 Liberty Drive
Bloomington, IN 47403
www.westbowpress.com
844-714-3454

Interior Image Credit: Myndi B. Smithers

ISBN: 978-1-9736-9138-9 (sc)
ISBN: 978-1-6642-0445-4(hc)
ISBN: 978-1-9736-9137-2 (e)

Print information available on the last page.

WestBow Press rev. date: 09/01/2020

Acknowledgments

I am deeply moved by all the individuals who assisted in making the book *Road Map Trough the Wilderness* a possibility. Unfortunately, there too many to mention. I am grateful to all who have supported me with their prayer, time, talents, and financial gifts. I could not have completed this without your assistance. Thank You!

My bride of nearly fifty years, Donna L. Claycomb, blesses me with untold hours of prayer, advice, support, and patience while unselfishly sacrificing the numerous hours I spent preparing this book.

I wish to thank Pastor William T. Sammons, Sr. who dedicated his life as pastor and bible teacher, contributing many of the concepts shared here today.

To Pastor Patrick A. Betts, the most anointed person I know, I offer gratitude for his example, counsel, and support. Your messages each Sunday morning bring power to my life.

To Pastor Marvin F. Jones, who is my confidant, offering much wisdom, compassion, and support. I give you my sincere thanks.

To Pastor Arthur T. Roxby III, Ph.D., confidant, best friend, deer hunter extraordinaire, Pastor Robert K. Muncy, Pastor H. John Betts, William E. Krieg, CPA, M. Daniel Herholdt, Jeffrey

G. East, Advisory Group members who have shared many untold hours in meetings and prayers. I am indebted to all, offering anointed wisdom and advice.

To Myndi B. Smithers and Lilah P. Claycomb for their amazing skills in creating RMTW images. Myndi sketched final drafts and Lilah created drawings of concepts, I express my gratitude.

To Ryan M. Claycomb, Ann G. Claycomb, Isaac A. Garcia, and Kelly A. Garcia, I offer heartfelt thanks for ongoing counsel and support.

To Sharea J. Adams for expertise applied in graphic design, I offer my gratitude.

Prologue

To His Credit

During my high school years, I lived on a dairy farm with my parents. Loving the outdoors and working daily with animals, I decided early to attend college as a dairy science major. In preparation, I knew I needed to pursue an academic curriculum while electing as many agriculture courses as possible. In tenth grade, I was told by my guidance counselor that a scheduling problem had occurred. If I wanted to attend agriculture classes, I had to sacrifice academic English classes or the academic math/science track. I could not pursue both. Considering the cattle could care less if my choice of words was appropriate, the math/science track was the obvious choice for my intended major in dairy science.

The SAT was a necessary step in my senior year to provide universities an accurate measure of academic skills and achievements. My math scores were acceptable for college entrance, but it was no surprise the creative writing exam score was a little less than disastrous. While other academic classmates learned skills for writing in their high school years, I sat through agriculture English courses, willingly sacrificing training skills of creative writing that I would need for a traditional college entrance scenario. With my English score of no significance, and my math score intact, I suspect my music audition was able to sway the entrance committee to accept my application. Yes. Ironically, I never applied to any university for dairy science but graduated with a Bachelor of Science Degree in Education as a music major.

Keeping in mind, the other freshman students had considerable experience in creative writing for several years previously in their high school academics, I studied none. Shortly after arrival at the university, I was not pleased when I discovered that I was required to take a creative writing class in my freshman year. The real emotion I experienced as I walked into the classroom the first day was pure terror. I was not only out of my comfort level but also out of my league. On the first day, while providing an overview of the course for the semester, the professor indicated that she would be commenting only on our papers submitted throughout the course. There would be no grades given on the homework. However, to determine our final grade, a ten-page research paper would be written at the end of the semester.

Although I made some progress throughout the course, I still was lacking significantly in creative writing skills. Late in the class, the professor explained more in detail, giving her students instruction and guidelines on this now infamous research paper we were required to write. The topic was about a hanging in England that occurred hundreds of years ago. This topic was quite familiar to her since she had chosen it to write her doctoral thesis. She even traveled to England for research in preparation for a book she later published on the subject. She knew most everything about this event that occurred centuries before. I knew nothing. She also made clear a truth that came to my mind nearly every day that I walked into the classroom. Any paper earning a grade of D or less meant a student would have to repeat the course. This truth enabled me to experience every physical and emotional feeling possible, resulting from the word dread. I knew I was doomed to repeat the course.

In preparation for my last paper at the end of the semester, I started my research, like every other student, by reading my professor's book. I also went to the university library, attempting to find additional books on the subject. I discovered too late, however, that nearly every student in the class did so as well. They had already checked out nearly every book on the topic. I realized I had to find additional information that was not readily available to establish some degree of recognition over the other students in my class. After an extensive search, I was able to locate several books on her topic at The Library of Congress in Washington, DC. Receiving them on loan, I was able to incorporate information into my writing that the other students did not have. After doing my best possible work, which was far from impressive, I finally came to complete and submit my work. Our professor informed us that once graded, she would not be returning these to us during class time. She would be meeting each person in her office individually to review our work in detail. Oh my! I would have to sit in front of her while she discussed my work. I could not tell you all the thoughts and emotions that went through my mind at that moment.

Upon arrival at her office, I saw my paper on her desk, neat and clean from any debris. There was absolutely nothing to distract her from that pathetic piece I submitted to her approximately a week earlier. The first words after greeting me were, "Mr. Claycomb; you have submitted a D paper." My heart sank as I thought of the many hours I endured, and the many more I would have to face next semester when I repeated this creative writing course. She continued, however, to speak, saying, "You are aware that the topic of this assignment is the same topic of the book I wrote for my doctoral thesis?" "Yes," I responded." She continued saying, "I have researched this topic thoroughly. However, you have found several books that I have failed to discover after working on this project for several years. I know you have done your research. I have given much thought about your final grade, considering the D paper you submitted. Based on your research efforts, however, I have decided you do not deserve a D as your final grade. Therefore, I have chosen to award you a final grade of C minus (minus) for the course. You will not have to repeat it." You mean I passed? I never heard of a C minus (minus) at that time. Being an educator in public schools for five years, I have never heard of a C minus (minus) since. I suspect before she read my paper that she never had either. Praise the Lord! Miracles do happen. I passed the course, I think. In any case, I did not have to repeat my required creative writing course.

I Corinthians 1:27(AMP), *"But God has selected [for His purpose] the foolish things of the world to shame the wise [revealing their ignorance], and God has selected [for His purpose] the weak things of the world to shame the things which are strong [revealing their frailty]."* As you read this book, please consider that *Road Map Through the Wilderness* not only reveals the frailty of the weak but also strengthens the *"frailty"* of the weak. That is, you and me in our wilderness struggles. It is impossible for me to understand the purposes of our Lord without His revelation. It is, therefore, impossible to fully know His purposes for this book. In authoring *Road Map Through the Wilderness,* however, I certainly can be categorized frail concerning my skills in writing. As for, *"the weak things of the world,"* possibly, I *"are"* one.

II Corinthians 12:9(AMP), *"for [My] power is being perfected [and is completed and shows itself most effectively] in [your] weakness. Therefore, I will all the more gladly boast in my weaknesses, so that the power of Christ [may completely enfold me and] may dwell in me."* Regarding the final draft of *Road Map Through the Wilderness*, consider I was just a young man who had no better sense than to ask repeatedly, "Lord, may I hear your voice?" The real miracle is that this book is being authored by someone who has few skills necessary to prepare and complete this text. All praise goes to our Lord!

In the beginning

I graduated from high school in the mid-'60s in a conservative Christian home in central-western Pennsylvania. Having no siblings, my parents gave me a solid foundation of love and support, for which I am very grateful. I grew up in a culture of an outdoorsman. Living on the farm gave me ample opportunity to enjoy the sun on my back and a breeze in my face, but the force driving me was much more in-depth. Even before we moved to the farm, our recreational time was beside or in a trout stream. Everything, however, became secondary to the deer hunt. If we were not hunting, we were spotlighting deer at night in the fields trying to locate big bucks and the largest concentration of deer. If we were not spotlighting deer, we were target practicing, trying to improve our hunting skills. If we were not shooting targets, we were visiting friends on Saturday nights telling stories of the hunt's failures and conquests in previous weeks, months, or years over a bowl of homemade ice cream. The culture was so prevalent in my region that the public schools would always close classes on the first day of buck season. This closure was because only a few came to school that day.

With the hippie mentality rapidly rising in the late 1960s,

I entered college, having my Christian values, finding my foundation of a family challenged. I observed free love offered and received by individuals of my generation, actions I had not understood or previously seen. I watched friends, individuals I did not expect to see, smoking pot, and taking drugs imitating a high that I experienced while outside in God's creation. Particularly disturbing to me was watching the nightly news posting pictures of Vietnam War protestors challenging the system with signs saying, among other things, "God is dead." One cold night about 11:00 PM, while lonely, sitting on a bench in the Oak Grove of the Indiana University of Pennsylvania, I pondered life in general, and my life specifically. I found an emptiness I had never known. Being challenged was the foundation I was given and thrived. I had to know with no doubt that God was real, that He was not dead. I needed to get back home to the farm.

Nestled on the side of a ridge are the farm buildings. Behind the house and barn was a hayfield sloping up and away from the house and barn. In previous years, I found solace while walking at night over the fields in the moonlight, while slowly strolling through the woods and hearing the cowbells tinkling in the distant still night. This night, I needed to meet God. This night, I decided I would seek him as I had never done before.

The air was crisp and cold as I stepped outside the farmhouse into the winter's night. As I walked through the hayfield behind the buildings, I could see the heavy frost collected on the blades of grass. The air was surprisingly still, as the crunch of each footstep broke the still winter night's silence. I slowly walked up the hill dimly lit by the full moon. After gathering my thoughts about halfway up the slope, I bowed on my knees, looked up into the night sky, and saw large puffy clouds floating slowly across the night sky in this winter eve's moonlight.

My prayer was simple. I asked the Lord to demonstrate in a way that I could not doubt, that He was authentic, and that He would do so that very night. I needed to know. As an afterthought, but quite important to me that night, I also asked that He show me that He knew who I was, that He knew me independently of all others. I imagined that He might appear and have a personal conversation with me there that crisp night, or somehow manifest Himself in the beautiful night sky illuminating angels around Him. Waiting on my knees, I fully expected to experience an encounter.

After about fifteen minutes of waiting, and not experiencing anything except pain in my knees, disappointed, I got up and continued my walk up the hill. Just over the hilltop, I sat down on a small mound of bare ground that a groundhog dug sometime earlier in a spring or summer long past. Sitting there pondering why there was no response from the Lord, and with the moonlight behind me, I was positioned far enough over the crest of the hill that it shadowed me in my position. The moon stood behind me as I looked down the backside of the ridge. In the still of the night, with no breeze moving, and in the shadows below me, I heard a step in the crisp cold grass. Shortly after, another, and yet another quiet movement made it evident that I was not alone. Each step that continued came closer and closer, which caused me to be concerned for my safety. Or could it possibly be ...? As the steps became quite close to my location, perhaps twenty feet, I made an unconscious reaction by clapping my hands just once. Immediately the footsteps stopped. After about ten minutes of silence, they slowly continued but were moving parallel to the hilltop line behind me instead of directly toward me. Several steps later revealed my visitors. A small herd of deer had been grazing in the hayfield and slowly moved into my exact location. No longer having concern about my well-being, still sitting in the shadow of the hilltop, I chose to stay and enjoy the moment's activity. Never had I an opportunity to be in the presence of a herd of deer to enjoy watching every move right in front of me. That alone was a memory I will never forget.

Being the consummate hunter, it occurred to me that if deer were in front of me; there also might be deer behind me. As I slowly turned around, I could feel the tension building inside me, hoping not to alert those in front of me. As my body swiveled approximately 180 degrees, I could not believe what I saw. As the moon rose, I could see, positioned precisely on the hill's crest behind me, the full moon. Silhouetted perfectly in the center of the moon was a huge male deer, a buck that stood broadside looking over his right shoulder directly at me. I could see his body, backlit by the bright full moon, was large with his antlers tall and wide having significant mass. I was amazed at what I was experiencing. In the shadows, I admired his majesty on the hilltop as he stood overseeing his herd while casually watching me between him and them.

It took several minutes after I started to walk back to the farmhouse to realize what exactly transpired on top of the hayfield just moments earlier. The closer I got to the house, the more I smiled, and the more I smiled, the louder I giggled. Realizing that the Lord answered my prayer in every detail, I pondered the events that just unfolded. What is the probability of a herd of deer coming in so close to me and not being alerted? What are the chances of me sitting precisely at the spot where the moon was perched on the hilltop at exactly the right moment that night? And what are the chances of all that happening when a beautiful buck stood precisely on the hill silhouetted, centered perfectly in the moon, and all shortly after I prayed. I did not see Jesus in the sky, illuminating the angels. He did not appear and speak to me. He gave this young outdoorsman something far better, a beautiful buck, silhouetted in the full moon, resting on the hilltop. I was in His presence, and He knew me!

CHAPTER 2

And the Floodgates Opened

Over the next approximately ten years, my relationship with the Lord developed slowly. My fraternity big brother visited my wife and me, arriving home from experiencing the Vietnam War sharing stories of salvation motivated by fear and terror. His witness of Jesus and stories of foxhole conversions enlightened me regarding a born-again commitment, a concept I had not previously understood or experienced. I heeded the words of Peter in **Acts 2:21(NKJV)** that says, *"And it shall come to pass that whoever calls on the name of the Lord shall be saved."* Several days after he left our home, about midnight, I found myself kneeling at the side of a small Delaware lake, asking the Lord to come into my life. I asked to walk in a relationship with Him, responding to the salvation message I had recently heard. That event was the catalyst that enabled my relationship with the Lord to blossom in my late twenties, influenced by Hal Lindsay's books on end times prophesies, including Jesus' second coming. My walk was focused, and my hunger for the Word became heightened.

Over the next ten years, my wife also walked into the Kingdom of God. We found ourselves sitting at the feet of then, Bible teacher Bill Sammons Sr., a gifted and anointed man of

God. During this season, in my mid-thirties, I was reading in Matthew's gospel about Jesus' wilderness experience. Seeing only a few verses written about this subject, I thought there had to be more than I was understanding. This time was crucial in His life. Several days later, I went back and reread it, having the same thoughts. What am I missing? Not understanding, I continued reading, being drawn back numerous times over the next several weeks and months.

One Saturday evening Bill Sammons Sr. approached me at Bible study and said, "I am not going to be here next week. How do you feel about sharing a message?" I quickly said yes, having no idea on what topic I would speak. Several days later, I fell into my periodic routine of reading Matthew's version of Jesus' wilderness walk. This time, however, was different. It was as if the floodgates opened regarding the scripture. I understood concepts and principals so quickly that I was unable to write fast enough to keep up.

Through the week, I organized what I now understood and presented it at Bible study the following Saturday night. Class attendees responded with great enthusiasm as I unfolded the truths I learned earlier in the week. Their response was quite positive. I could see this message touched a tender place of need in the hearts of the people attending that evening. The next morning at church service, enthused, I shared this message with the congregation who also responded with considerable interest. Over the years, this one teaching became the foundation of a two series message. The first is *Road Map Through the Wilderness,* which has developed into ten one to one and a half hour lessons. This book is an extension of those lessons. The second is named *It is Finished, but Not Yet Complete,* now seven lessons with several more to be written.

Over the next several years, I had several opportunities to share this message. After the initial illumination, *Road Map Through the Wilderness* developed into six segments. I was pleased to have the opportunity to present these on consecutive Wednesday nights at my new church that Bill Sammons now pastored. Knowing that I had never taught a Bible class before and being considerate of my feelings, my then Associate Pastor Rick Betts, tried to soften the impact of his anticipated dwindling attendance. He explained that it was common for class attendance to diminish over time. When the class increased the third week by Fifty percent, he decided to attend.

Again I shared while attending another church. The response of the attendees was quite amazing. Considering all the enthusiastic comments about the text, I believed this was a message of opportunity in the context of kingdom significance. I prayerfully decided not to continue taking this message out to the church body prematurely in the flesh and miss the Lord's leading, miss His best. In prayer, I said, "Lord, if this is you, I will commit myself to get this message out to the masses, but I ask that you open doors. This wilderness teaching appears to touch most people who have heard it. There are too many tasks to do, and too many skills that I do not have. I will wait for you to lead."

While I waited, weeks became months, months became years, and years became decades. All the while, the Lord kept expanding this theme. In doing so, I only wrote down what I heard. It originated from word studies, numerous personal experiences, sermons in the pulpit, and many teachings, the message slowly developed over time. It was expanded through deep heartache, listening to television sermons, while praying, and all from a supernatural illumination of the Word that originated now more than thirty-five years ago.

CHAPTER 3

Launch Time

Approximately ten years ago, The thought occurred to me that most of my adult life was involved in writing and organizing this message and that the Lord had not initiated any activity to introduce it to the church or general public. After waiting all these years, one quiet night during my prayer time, I asked Him this question. "Lord, you are not going to let me take *Road Map Through the Wilderness* to my grave, are you?" In that very same prayer, I spoke the words of **Isaiah 6:8(NIV)** saying, *"Here am I, send me,"* committing myself to whatever and wherever the Lord wanted to take this message.

During this season, I also realized the amount of work needed to complete this project was huge. I had many family and business responsibilities with little time to do them. Besides, I did not have the skills required to complete many of those tasks needed to get this message to the public; video, website, marketing, writing a book, and others. I did not have the resources that were needed. Now, approximately ten years later, I can testify that the Lord has provided every job, every skill, and somehow every need. In the future, I have no doubt the Lord will continue to do the same.

It was not long after this prayer that the following event

occurred that launched *Road Map Through the Wilderness* into motion. I received a call from a gentleman who had been faithful in calling me to pray for a significant need that I had for a prolonged time. This gentleman worked for a vendor that provided a product offering Christian values that I offered to my clients, The Timothy Plan Mutual Funds. As we chatted after prayer, he asked me if I was planning to attend the annual Christian conference for our industry. It was to start Thursday of the following week. After checking my calendar, I explained that attending would not be possible. My wife and I were traveling for a mini-vacation and would be arriving home on Wednesday, the day before the conference started. It would be impossible to prepare to fly out the next morning. We were returning from a trip to Disney World in Orlando, Florida, and needed rest, time to unpack and pack again before we could embark on another engagement. Later, after we dismissed the topic, I asked him where they were meeting. His reply immediately caused my kingdom antennas to rise. Orlando was the city where the meeting would occur. Possibly it was not a coincidence that we were flying out of the same airport the day before the conference started. Perhaps this might be God orchestrating this discussion for us to attend. My reply to him was that I would consider staying in Orlando for the event. I promised to go home for lunch and talk to my wife and get back with him with our decision.

This gentleman and I ended our conversation, and an hour later, I arrived at the house for lunch. My wife was agreeable to the travel extension; however, there was an issue about the extra funds needed. We would incur an additional fee to change our flight tickets, a fee for the conference, and of course, a big-ticket for the 5-star hotel where we would be staying. After some calculations, we determined we would not be able to attend. We did not have the spare cash to extend our trip. I went back to the office and called this brother in the Lord and told him regrettably; we would not be attending. His original call to me was at approximately ten-thirty AM. My returned call was about one-thirty PM. Several hours later, my assistant walked into my office and gave me an envelope with my name. She said that someone walked into the office, gave it to her, and left the office. Puzzled, I opened the envelope and discovered a check payable to me precisely for the amount we needed for expenses to attend the conference, unexpected, without notice, and precisely on time.

I immediately called my wife with the first words out of my mouth, saying, "You are not going to believe this." After I explained, we agreed that the Lord had something for us there and that we should attend. After the conference, it was obvious the Lord had given both direction and motivation to initiate the development of *Road Map Through the Wilderness*. There were many occurrences similar over the years of the Lord's leading, too numerous to mention. All illustrate the Lord's leading and provision. Over the years, with all the steps needed to complete this project, I had no understanding of the next step until I completed or nearly completed the current project. Only at the end of each did He illuminate my next task and provide the persons and provisions needed to complete it. In doing so, He also confirmed His instructions.

CHAPTER 4

Concept Introduction

There are two primary themes in this wilderness message. *Series 1, Road Map Through the Wilderness* is a message of hope, deliverance, identity, authority, and empowerment. It is an opportunity to receive ministry unto restoration from the Lord. It is God's direction, by Jesus' example, guiding us on how to walk through and out of our wilderness experience. He wants you to know that He understands His bride, you, are experiencing trials, temptations, pain, despair, fear, anger, and many other concerns that are challenging you. His message to you is that He knows you are there and has given you the provision to get out. You do not have to stay there! *He wants to minister to you.*

What is your need today? Take a quiet moment, look inside yourself, and answer these questions honestly.

1. Are you caught up in a wilderness experience and do not know how to get out?
2. Do you know what your specific purpose in life is?
3. Do you feel you are still short of where God wants you to be and can not get there?
4. Do you feel so lost, so cut off, so alone?

5. Does your Christian life lack direction?
6. Is your life stuck or stagnant in a wilderness walk?
7. Are you spiritually disabled?
8. Are you dry in your spirit, worn by your walk?
9. Are you tired of just struggling to maintain?
10. Do you wonder why there is not more victory in your life?
11. Do you desire more power in your Christian walk?

Road Map Through the Wilderness will answer these questions and many more. If these questions address your need, describing where you are today, this message is undoubtedly for you. Jesus in *Road Map Through the Wilderness* will show you how to get out of your wilderness experience. The Father has a plan for you in your wilderness walk.

Mike Murdock says in his daily online post, *Morning Motivation,* "Expect a turnaround. Your feelings are not your life. Your worst circumstances today are subject to change. God is stepping into the arena of your life. He is turning the tide in your favor. You are not as far from a miracle as it first appears. The difference in seasons is the instruction you are willing to follow." **Isaiah 40:4-5(NKJV),** *"Every valley shall be exalted, and every mountain and hill shall be made low: and the crooked shall be made straight, and the rough places plain: And the glory of the Lord shall be revealed, and all flesh shall see it together: for the mouth of the Lord hath spoken it."*

Second, He wants you to understand He is giving you, the church, an opportunity to minister just like Jesus. Series 2 – *It is Finished, but Not Yet Complete,* is a message of implementation, an exhibition of engagement, and an opportunity that He has created for you. That is, to enable you to fulfill what He has created you to be in a partnership with Him. It is God's Word on how He desires to work through the church, implementing power by authority, to place Jesus' enemies as footstools under His feet.

The church has undoubtedly taken Jesus' lead and walked as lambs and servants in the natural. Could this be the time when the Father calls the church to follow Jesus' lead to take dominion as Lions of Judah in the Spirit? In **John 14:12(ESV)**, Jesus says, *"Truly, truly, I say to you, he who believes in me will also do the works that I do; and greater works than these will he do because I am going to the Father."* Yes, there have been remnants, but many of the church has yet to fulfill this prophecy. Could the time be now? Darkness is getting darker in our world. The church must get brighter. Satan wants us to go in the wilderness and stay there. The Father wants us to go in for a while, learn a few things, implement, and come out in the power of the Holy Spirit, anointed, and sent. Too many of us, as did I, find ourselves in wilderness experiences, do not know how to get out, why we should get out, or what to do when we do get out. He has a plan for you. Therefore, let us take His advice in **I Peter 5:6-7(NKJV)** and, *"... therefore humble yourselves under the mighty hand of God, that He may exalt you in due time, casting all your care upon Him, for He cares for you.*

CHAPTER 5

Reasons for Problems

Scripture tells us there are at least four reasons we have problems. **Romans 6:23(NIV)**, *"For the wages of sin is death, but the free gift of God is eternal life in Christ Jesus our Lord."* Death certainly is problematic, whether it is physical death, spiritual death, relational death, or any other death. We can say we have problems resulting from being in sin, that is, out of God's will. What we earn is death.

   Jonah 1:10-12(NRSV), *"Then the men were even more afraid, and said to him, 'What is this that you have done!' For the men knew that he was fleeing from the presence of the Lord, because he had told them so. Then they said to him, 'What shall we do to you, that the sea may quiet down for us? For the sea was growing more and more tempestuous.' He said to them, 'Pick me up and throw me into the sea; then the sea will quiet down for you; for I know it is because of me that this great storm has come upon you.' Then the men were even more afraid, and said to him, 'What is this that you have done!'* The sailors were terrified. This great storm was about to break the ship apart. The difficulties they were experiencing had nothing to do with their choices or their behavior. Their life was in danger because they were close to Jonah in the ship. He was the one who was out of God's will. Therefore, like these sailors, we also can have problems when we are close to someone out of God's will.

Ephesians 6:12(NKJV), *"For we do not wrestle against flesh and blood, but against principalities, against powers, against the rulers of the darkness of this age,[a] against spiritual hosts of wickedness in the heavenly places."* The operative word here is we. We, the church, have problems because we are wrestling with principalities, powers, rulers of the darkness of this age, and spiritual hosts. Why? It is because we are in God's will. Darkness will come against us to combat our walk, our relationship, our identity with Christ, and all the fruit resulting from a relationship with Him. We, therefore, will have problems when we are in God's will.

Job 1:12(NIV), "The Lord said to Satan, *"Very well, then, everything he has is in your power, but on the man himself do not lay a finger."* Satan came to the Father, saying he did not think Job was as loyal as the Father thought. **Job 1:12(NIV)** is the Father's answer to Satan. By this example, we may also find ourselves under the influence of Satan's direct attack. That certainly will be problematic.

In this text, we will focus on three of these, having problems when in God's will, wrestling with dark powers, and Satan's direct attack.

CHAPTER 6

Your True Identity

In **John 17:4(AMPC)** Jesus says to the Father, "*I have glorified You down here on the earth by completing the work that You gave Me to do.*" What exactly is that work? In **Isaiah 61:1-3(AMP)**, we see the prophecy of the ministry of the Messiah, Jesus. "*The Spirit of the Lord God is upon me because the Lord has **anointed** and commissioned me to bring good news to the humble and afflicted. He has **sent** me to bind up [the wounds of] the brokenhearted, to proclaim release [from confinement and condemnation] to the [physical and spiritual] captives and freedom to prisoners, to proclaim [a]the favorable year of the Lord, b]and the day of vengeance and retribution of our God to grant [consolation and joy] to those who mourn in **Zion**—to give them an ornament (a garland or diadem) of beauty instead of ashes, the oil of joy instead of mourning, the garment [expressive] of praise instead of a heavy, burdened, and failing spirit—that they may be called oaks of righteousness [lofty, strong, and magnificent, distinguished for uprightness, justice, and right standing with God], the planting of the Lord, that He may be glorified.*

    www.dictionary.com defines Zion, "(in Christian thought) the heavenly city or kingdom of heaven, the Christian Church." He is speaking of you, the church. You are spiritual, Zion. He wants to give you, *"beauty instead of ashes, oil of joy instead of mourning, the garment of praise instead of a heavy burdened and failing heart."* That is your identity. That is the Father's heart toward you, to bless you, that you may be called, *"Oaks of Righteousness; lofty, strong, and magnificent, distinguished for uprightness, justice, and right standing with God."* Look inside yourself. Do you feel like oaks today? Have you chosen that identity? Is that your experience? Lord, help me to see myself through your eyes rather than seeing myself through my own eyes? Identity! It is all about your identity in Christ given by the Father! Do I see myself as the Lord sees me? Do I see myself as who I am, who He created me to be? This scripture is the prophecy of the ministry of the Messiah, and Jesus says, *"it is finished"* **John 19:30(NKJV).**

I have a cousin who has been well-rooted in the Lord for many years. He and I have a unique relationship in that we like to tease each other with sarcasm. The goal is to get a little dig on the other, and then we laugh together. The other would return the joke as the laughter continued throughout our lives. Many years ago, I observed others giving alter ministry with amazing results. People were getting saved, healed of physical ailment, relational breakdowns restored, and inner turmoil released. Although this was relatively early in my faith walk, I also had the opportunity to pray with people at the altar with less than stellar results. Somewhat confused, I shared with my cousin my disappointment at my appeared failure at altar ministry. Joking, but in love, he said, "So, who put you in charge of Holy Spirit ministry?" He was saying, who is to say that is your ministry? I then understood that healing of diseases and casting out unclean spirits may not have been my gift. Through him, the Lord was showing me; it is not about healing alone. It is all about power and anointing in the ministry the Lord gives me. For the church now, the question is this. Considering the gifts that I have, am I walking in them to their maximum? Or more accurately, why am I not adequate or less than adequate in whatever gifts the Lord has given me? What is missing?

What are the Father's thoughts on this? Where does the Father want us to be? **Psalm 110:1-2(AMP)** says, *"The Lord (father) says to my Lord (Messiah): Sit at my right hand."* When do you think that moment occurred? It was Jesus' arrival in heaven, just after His ascension from the earth, post-resurrection. **Mark 16:19(NIV)**, *"After the Lord Jesus had spoken to them, he was taken up into heaven, and he sat at the right hand of God."* Jesus ascended to heaven arriving in the throne room. He was invited by the Father, to sit at His right hand. **Romans 8:34(NKJV)** *"Who is he who condemns? It is Christ who died, and further also is risen, who is even at the right hand of God; who also makes intercession for you."* I ask, if Jesus is on the throne of power, at the right hand of the Father, and I am proclaiming Christ, why am I not walking in power and anointing?

Steve Keller, past Senior Pastor, Kempsville Presbyterian Church, Virginia Beach, Virginia, spoke of identity about this. **I Peter 1:1-2(AMPC)**, *"Peter, an apostle (a special messenger) of Jesus Christ, [writing] to the elect exiles of the dispersion scattered (sowed) abroad in Pontus, Galatia, Cappadocia, Asia, and Bithynia, Who were chosen and foreknown by God the Father and consecrated (sanctified, made holy) by the Spirit to be obedient to Jesus Christ (the Messiah) and to be sprinkled with [His] blood: May grace (spiritual blessing) and peace be given you in increasing abundance[that spiritual peace to be realized in and through Christ freedom from fears, agitating passions, and moral conflicts]."* Here we see Peter writing to a group of people who are not in their homeland. *Dictionary.com* defines the word exile as, "prolonged separation from one's country or home, as by force of circumstances." They are scattered and located among many foreign places, exiled. But Peter says here they are also chosen and foreknown by God, sanctified. The *Merriam-Webster Dictionary* defines the word sanctified, "to set aside to a sacred purpose."

We, too, find ourselves in a foreign land, here on earth. We are not in our home. Our home is in heaven. **Hebrews 11:13-14, 16(NKJV)**, *"These all died in faith, not having received the promises, but having seen them were assured of them, embraced them, and confessed that they were strangers and pilgrims on the earth. For those who say, such things declare plainly that they seek a homeland. But now they desire a better place that is a, heavenly country."* As we speak, mansions and streets of gold are in the process of being prepared for us. Heaven is under construction. We tend to forget, being here, that the Lord has chosen us. We tend to forget the Lord foreknows us. And hearing what people say of us, what people think of us as Christians, we do not feel chosen, or foreknown, or sanctified by God. But in this scripture, the Lord is telling us that we are not second-class citizens. The world system would tell us that. Darkness tries to convince us of that. Those of spiritual darkness try to take our identity away as bonified heirs to the kingdom of Heaven. Understand that Hell's inhabitants and those influenced by them are lying to us. We are not, and you are not who the world has led you to believe. Know that you are complete in Jesus, not less than complete in Him, as the world would say. The Father wants us to know that as His chosen ones, we are set apart by Jesus. None of this walk, none of this world is of any importance if we do not have our identity in Christ properly understood; if we do not know who we are, whose we are, and why we are. We cannot be the person He created us to be if we do not know who we are. Therefore, we are ineffective or at least less effective in our role as Jesus' brother/sister and the Father's son/ daughter. And if we cannot be the person He has created us to be, we are ineffective or at least less effective in our role as Jesus' brother/sister and the

Father's son/daughter. If we are ineffective or less than effective, we have no power or little power. And if we are ineffective or less than effective with no power or little power, we are not fulfilled as Christians. Therefore, we are unable to walk in the Father's will in **Isaiah 61:3(NKJV)**, mentioned above being less than fulfilled, less than oaks referenced in this scripture! And I see so many people not fulfilled. Do you know who you are, whose you are, and why you are? The Lord is speaking of the wilderness here. He is speaking of identity with the opportunity to be fulfilled. That is His heart for you!

What is the effect of that identity on you? **Job 25:2(NKJV)** says, *"Dominion and fear belongs to Him."* That is to say; dominion belongs to God. **John 17:2(NKJV)** says, *"as you have given Him authority over all flesh."* The Father gives dominion to Jesus. In **John 17:9-10(NKJV)**, *"I do not pray for the world but for those whom You have given Me, for they are Yours. All Mine are Yours, and all Yours are Mine, and I am glorified in them."* We see Jesus praying for the disciples. **John 17:20(NKJV)**, *"I do not pray for these alone, but also for those who will believe in me through their word."* Jesus is praying for you!" **Psalm 8:4-6(NKJV)**, *"What is man that You are mindful of him, and the son of man that you visit him? For you have made him a little lower than the angels, and You have crowned him with glory and honor. You have made him to have dominion over the works of Your hands; You have put all things under his feet."* Dominion, ruling over the earth and His kingdom here on earth, has been given to us by the Father. The Father passes His authority through Jesus to us in **II Corinthians 5:21(NKJV)**, *"For He made Him who knew no sin to be sin for us, that we might become the righteousness of God in Him."* Since Jesus took on our identity and became sin, our nature, we are enabled to take on His, the righteousness of God. The Father has passed spiritual authority to Jesus, and now Jesus passes spiritual authority to us. Thus, we become the righteousness of God. It is a wonderous trade. We can now walk in dominion because He has predestined us to conform to Jesus' image, which will be discussed later. Because He has predestined us to conform to Jesus' image, we too can walk in dominion. That is the Father's plan for you. Our Lord wants us to know that we can.

The world has lied to us. This world tells us how to think and what to do. The world says we are nobody unless we produce. They would have us believe we are fake. But you are not who the world has led you to believe. You are the righteousness of God in Jesus.

Please understand you have available NOTHING LESS than the authority of NONE OTHER than the Father Himself. Our culture has attempted to make many of us in the church less than powerful. As darkness presses on, too many of us have had our senses dulled over time. Our Christian identity is deteriorating. The influence of darkness is numbing us both in our culture and our individual lives. Many of those in the kingdom of God are wounded spiritually as the advance of darkness moves forward. Darkness would have you stay in your wilderness and become less effective, ultimately becoming ineffective.

Unfortunately, many of us have lost that identity in Christ, or as some individuals, never really have obtained it. That is our identity as a child of God and a brother/sister of none other than the Messiah! You still may say, "I am not authentic; I am not legitimate." I do not have the Father's bloodline in my veins." The blood flowing down the cross says differently. That is why you take communion. God has made you in His image. Jesus died for you because you are valuable. The Lord God almighty entrusts to you His authority, and it starts in the wilderness!

CHAPTER 7

Can We Really Do That?

Acts 5:15-16(NKJV), "*so that they brought the sick out into the streets and laid them on beds and couches, that at least the shadow of Peter passing by might fall on some of them.*" Let us look at the dynamics here. People were carrying their beds and couches into the streets. This activity is a most unusual scenario in any city or town, then or now. People were waiting for Peter to walk down their street near them. We can consider this was not just one event. It says people were taking their infirmed into the, "*streets.*" This event was happening throughout the whole city. Peter did not decide to take a walk down a street only one sunny afternoon. The Holy Spirit was moving throughout the entire city for a season. We can determine they were hoping that Peter's shadow would fall on them or their loved ones. The question that screams for an answer is this. Why? Why were people disrupting their homes? Why were they carrying their infirmed into the streets? Why were their beds and couches placed in the streets throughout Jerusalem? Why were they motivated to have Peter's shadow fall on them? The answer is obvious. The Lord was performing miraculous manifestations of Holy Spirit signs and wonders. People were getting healed. Lives were getting changed. There was a stir in Jerusalem at that time.

"Also a multitude gathered from surrounding cities to Jerusalem, bringing sick people and those who were tormented by unclean spirits." In those days, people did not have cell phones. They did not have texting. They did not have nightly news. They certainly did not have the internet. The only way information passed from city to city was by word of mouth. That took time to evolve. Considering preparation time and travel time from their city to Jerusalem, to finally arrive, did not happen quickly. Let us understand this is not a small move of God. The Holy Spirit was manifesting in a mighty wave of miracles and doing so for a long time. Those who were tormented by unclean spirits and those who were sick were all there. This scripture says, *"a multitude gathered,"* and, *"THEY WERE ALL HEALED!"*

This magnificent demonstration of Holy Spirit power was not the first time it happened. **Mark 6:54-56(NKJV)**, *"And when they came out of the boat, immediately the people recognized Him, ran through the whole surrounding region, and began to carry about on beds those who were sick to wherever they heard He was. Wherever He entered into villages, cities, or the country, they laid the sick in the marketplaces, and begged Him that they might touch the hem of his garment and as many that touched Him WERE MADE WELL!"* This scripture is speaking of Jesus. We can see that Peter's results in Jerusalem were not the first time these very same results occurred. We can see the people responded to the same power exhibited by Jesus manifested in the same way. They came from the whole region. They lay the sick in public places, hoping they might connect somehow to be benefactors of that incredible power exhibited. Peter has picked up the mantle, with the same authority as Jesus had, and demonstrated the very same power of the Holy Spirit, the same way Jesus did.

We will hear much about **Romans 8:29(NKJV)**, *"We are*

predestined to conform to the image of His Son." We will learn what will happen and only occur when choosing to place our identity in the Father as son and daughter and the Son of God as brother and sister.

The Father passed that same anointing to the Son of God, Jesus. Jesus then gave that anointing to a son of man, Peter, who earlier became a man of God. **II Corinthians 13:10 (NKJV)**, *"Therefore I write these things, being absent, lest being present I should use sharpness, according to the authority which the Lord has given me.*" Peter was born with the same Adamic nature as you and me. We are all born into a sinful nature, but that same sin nature passed on from Adam to us. Each of us inherits it.

As an observer, I can easily understand that the Son of God could manifest these miracles, but a Holy Spirit manifestation through Peter in Jerusalem is the real miracle. This same power and anointing, with the Father's authority, now has been exhibited unto full manifestation through the sinner man, Peter. And now, even though you also have inherited the Adamic nature, the nature of sinner man, you also have the same opportunity to have the full manifestation of the Holy Spirit, anointing, and power as Peter. As mentioned earlier, the Bible says Jesus went into the wilderness, *"being filled with the Holy Spirit"* in **Luke 4:4(NKJV)**. He *"returned in the power of the Spirit"* **Luke4:14(NKJV)**. Something happened in there! We can now see that the Father has also predestined you, sinner man and woman born in the Adamic nature, to receive the same anointing unto POWER!

If the Father has predestined us to conform to His image, do we experience that power today, seeing all people healed from a myriad of diseases and dark influences? Do we see that same power in our world to the extent that Peter and Jesus ministered? I have been to services that Holy Spirit ministry was evident. I have been to church services with no evidence of Holy Spirit ministry and to one service that had no Word offered. I have never been to a church service where they were all healed. Why is that? There is a hurting world out there! The world needs to receive ministry now with the same power demonstrated by Peter and Jesus. Are we not predestined to conform to the image of Jesus, as well?

That is an honest question. Do we not have the same Holy Spirit, the same Jesus, the same Father as Peter, Paul, and other New Testament saints? Possibly, God does not want to minister to people anymore, or perhaps He wants to minister to fewer people, or maybe the Holy Spirit does not move like that today? No! No! And No!

On the cross, Jesus said, "It is finished." He completed everything He was asked by the Father to do. He dealt with Satan in the wilderness. He healed the sick, and He dealt with the demonic after the wilderness. He preached the Father's Word, and He set the captives free. Jesus is our example. **Hebrews 13:8(NLT)** says, *"Jesus Christ is the same yesterday, today and forever."* He has the same heart for humankind now that He had then. He desires to bless, demonstrated by Peter and Jesus. If He wanted to change the lives of a multitude then, He desires to minister to the lives of multitudes now.

Using the baseball method of calculating a batting average, a player getting on base 300 times out of 1,000 has a batting average of 300. A player who might get on base 1000 times out of 1,000 times at bat has a batting average of 1,000. We can say then that Jesus and Peter were " batting" 1,000 because scripture says, *"He healed them all"* **Matthew4:24(TLB)**. Why then are there no great ministries in vast numbers in amazing ways demonstrating power and anointing today? The need is indeed here. Why are we not batting 1000?

Today the need is to enable Holy Spirit power to go forth in magnitude. Let us understand there are no great men and women of God, but only men and women with a great God. Let us know then that every Christian alive is a candidate for that same power and anointing that Jesus and the early church had. Does that mean you will get there? No, but it means you can. Knowing that we are to conform to His image, and knowing we are in the same sinner man category as the saints of the Bible, why do we not see much evidence of the same power and anointing with the same magnitude and frequency, as seen in the Bible? Why do we not walk with Spirit power like Jesus and Peter? Why then was Peter of Acts batting 1,000 and us batting…?

We are going to learn about a *Road Map Through the Wilderness*. There is a walk, a path that brings authority, power, and the anointing called forth in **Psalm 110:1-2**. It is all found in a *Road Map Through the Wilderness*, which demonstrates to us how we, the church, will walk in **John 14:12(NKJV)** where Jesus says, *"Most assuredly, I say to you, he who believes in Me, the works that I do he will do also; and greater works than these he will do, because I go to My Father."* Can I get out of my wilderness? The answer is an absolute yes! Can you get out of your wilderness? Yes, you can! Can you bat 1000? You can believe it. Jesus, Peter, and the new testament saints demonstrated it. Jesus walked the road. We see the Road Map. That is the story we will hear.

CHAPTER 8

Seven Steps

There are seven steps to Jesus' walk through the wilderness.

1. Jesus heard the **Father's words** immediately after being baptized. The Father proclaimed Jesus' identity as Son at the Jordan River with the Holy Spirit descending upon Him.

2. In the wilderness, Jesus heard **opposition** to the Father's Words.

3. Jesus had to **ponder/think** about the two scenarios presented before Him.

4. Jesus had to **choose** whom He was going to place His identity; the Father or Satan.

5. Jesus had to **submit** Himself to the identity He chose.

6.   Jesus received the Father's **authority**.

7.   Jesus placed that authority into action. He **engaged** Satan in battle, putting the Father's authority into action.

I. Hearing the Father's Words - Matthew 3:16(NKJV), *"When He had been baptized, Jesus came up immediately out of the water; and behold, the heavens were opened to Him, and He saw the Spirit of God descending like a dove and alighting on Him."*

THE FATHER'S WORDS

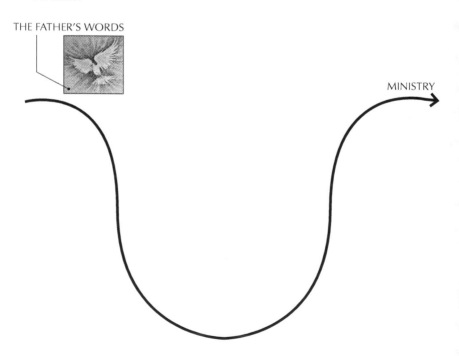

MINISTRY

If there was any question who Jesus was before His baptism, there certainly was none after. Jesus heard with His natural ears, and He processed this with His natural mind what the Father declared. He understands, intellectually, who He is. Note that the Father did not say You are my beloved Son. He was not speaking to Jesus only. His proclamation was to the world. In **Matthew 3:17(NKJV)**, the Father proclaims, *"This is my Son in whom I am well pleased."* Using the word *"this,"* He was speaking to others. His announcement resonated throughout that day and throughout history to this day and will continue until he comes again, splitting open the eastern sky. The result of that event gives Jesus His identity as the Son of God. Thus, the first step of Jesus' road through the wilderness is hearing the Father's Word after baptism and receiving His identity. At this moment, we see the Holy Spirit descending on Jesus like a dove that brings on a new concept not generally recognized until that day; the fullness of the Holy Spirit and all He gives. Jesus now has an identity as Son and the presence of the Holy Spirit in His life. The equation is now complete. All is in place. Jesus is ready for ministry, or is He?

By receiving the Holy Spirit, Jesus now has every spiritual tool He needs to go into ministry. His spiritual toolbox was full, but the Father did not immediately call Him to fulfill the prophecy of the Messiah in **Isaiah 61**. Jesus, being full of the Holy Spirit, leaving the Jordan region, got lost and found Himself in the wilderness. Is that correct? No, of course not. Does it say, Jesus, walking away from the Jordan River, was approached by the devil who enticed Him into the wilderness? That is not correct, either. **Luke 4:1(NKJV)** says, *"Then Jesus, being filled with the Holy Spirit, returned from the Jordan and was led by the Spirit [a]into the wilderness."* By leading Jesus into the wilderness, the Holy Spirit had something in mind.

What could the Holy Spirit have been thinking? Do I understand that the Father sent Jesus in the wilderness to tempt

Him? Could it possibly be that there was a purpose for Jesus' wilderness experience? There must have been a reason. If the Holy Spirit had led Jesus into the wilderness, it must have been necessary. The Holy Spirit and the Father must have had an agenda for Jesus to be there. Yes, God wanted Him there! We can only conclude there was a purpose in being tempted in Jesus experiencing the wilderness. In **Luke 4:14(NKJV)** we learn that, *"Jesus returned in the power of the Spirit.* This truth now revealed is crucial for our understanding as we maneuver through and out of our wilderness walk. Jesus went in the wilderness filled with the Holy Spirit but came out empowered with the Holy Spirit. Something amazing happened in there!

II. Opposing Word - It was not a coincidence that Satan also arrived. His words help us determine why he came at that specific time and that place. **Luke 4:3(AMPC),** *"Then the devil said to Him, If You are the Son of God, order this stone to turn into a loaf [of bread]."*

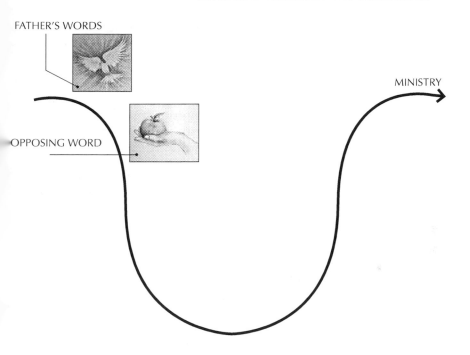

FATHER'S WORDS

MINISTRY

OPPOSING WORD

Focusing on that little word *if,* we can discover the answer. Understand that just before Jesus' arrival, the Father declared to the world at the Jordan River in **Matthew 3:17(NKJV)**, "*This is my beloved son.*" Jesus already knows who He is. The Father just gave His identity to Him.

What then is Satan trying to do? The answer is simple. He is attempting to place doubt in Jesus' mind. We can now see the second place in Jesus' wilderness walk: He heard opposition to the Father's Words by Satan. The Father says, "*you are my Son.*" Satan's message is, if You are His Son. He is challenging Jesus' identity as the Son of God. Our wilderness walk is the same process Jesus faced. God puts our identity in place first by speaking His Word to us. We might hear the Word of salvation spoken from the pulpit, from an acquaintance, and perhaps on television as the spoken Word. Or we might discover it in the Bible, the written Word. After we hear that Word and choose our

Lord for salvation, the Holy Spirit will lead us into the wilderness. Satan arriving will present an opposing word, always something contrary to what the Father says, all to get us to doubt or question our identity as the Father's son or daughter.

III. Give Thought - This conflict causes us to give thought. We need to ponder *in* our minds what we just heard, thus, what we should choose. **I John 1:5(NKJV)**, *"This is the message which we have heard from Him and declare to you, that God is light and in Him, there is no darkness at all."* Where there is light, there can be no darkness. We cannot choose to accept some of what Satan says and some of what the Father says. Consider the options carefully before you make a choice. Are we going to choose to place our identity in the Father, or are we going to place it in Satan? Are we going to walk as a son/daughter of God, or are we going to walk as a son/daughter of Satan? It can only be one or the other. There can be no middle ground. We must give thought to the two opposing positions.

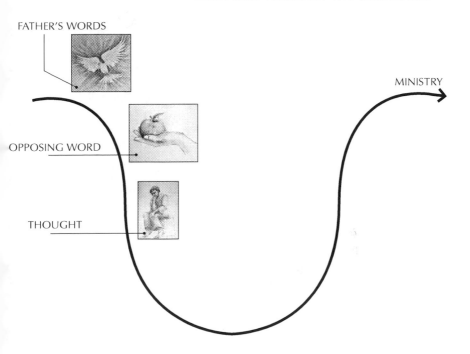

FATHER'S WORDS

MINISTRY

OPPOSING WORD

THOUGHT

IV. Choose - It was at the riverbank where God told Jesus He was His Son. It was in the wilderness where Satan challenged the Father's words. Jesus had to make His own decision for Himself because God is a gentleman. He did not force His identity on Jesus. Nor will He force His identity on you. It is the wilderness where we choose ourselves, our identity as a son or daughter of the Father or a brother or sister of the Messiah. Our wilderness walk is the same process Jesus faced. The Holy Spirit will lead us into the wilderness with Satan arriving with an opposing word, always something contrary to what the Father says, to get us to doubt or question our identity that the Father's Word gives us. Indeed, the Father encourages us to make the right decision in **Deuteronomy 30:19b(NKJV)**, *"that I have set before you life and death, blessing and cursing; therefore choose life, that both you and your descendants may live."* His heart is for you to choose life and blessing.

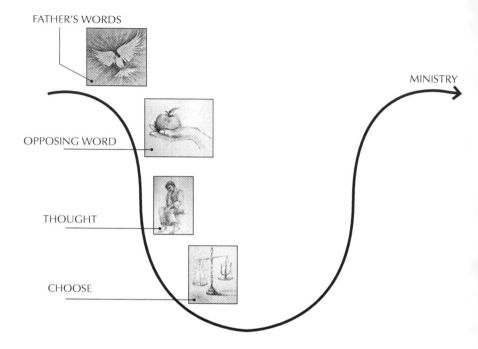

V. Submit and Obey - In **James 4:7(NKJV)** the Lord says, *"Therefore submit to God. Resist the devil, and he will flee from you."* It is one thing to make a choice. It is quite another to submit yourself to the one whom you choose.

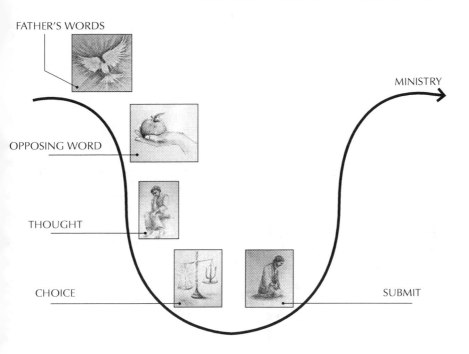

FATHER'S WORDS

MINISTRY

OPPOSING WORD

THOUGHT

CHOICE

SUBMIT

Exodus 23:22(NKJV), *"But if though indeed obey His voice and do all that I speak: then I will be an enemy to your enemies and an adversary to your adversaries."* It is in my obedience, where my enemies become the Lord's enemies. It is in my obedience where my adversaries become the Lord's adversaries. Obedience is the fruit of submission. Submission is the catalyst of obedience. If we submit to someone, obedience is the natural response. If we are not submitted, we, therefore, do not obey. If I am not obedient in my wilderness walk, I am fighting my enemies alone.

I must admit that obedience has been one of my most difficult tasks in life. Too often, I have disappointed myself and the Lord, of which I am sure. By sharing some of my struggles and observing similarities in yourself, you might find understanding in the implementation of obedience in your own life.

    1.   If I do not obey out of submission, I tend to submit when I hurt, enough. Then I obey. My obedience is not for the

right motive, and I have failed the Lord's test even though I submit. It is out of selfishness.

2. I do not submit if I am not in fear. I submit when I am fearful enough. Then I obey. It is not for the right reason, and I have failed our Lord's test. It is because of selfishness.

3. I do not obey when I am comfortable. I submit when I am uncomfortable. Then I obey. It is not for the right motive, and I have failed our Lord's test. It is because of selfishness.

4. I do not obey when I am too busy. I submit when I am not too busy, only when convenient, then I obey. It is because of selfishness.

5. If I have not been obedient to His will, I obey for personal reasons. I obey to satisfy, to comfort my hurting flesh. It is not for the right reasons, and I have failed His test.

Still, when I am obedient to satisfy my flesh, not out of love and dedication to the Father, He is always faithful, always reacting in love, He restores when asked for forgiveness. It is called grace. Lord, please forgive me? It is called unmerited love. Lord, thank you for your forgiveness. Is it not amazing?

It is not if I submit that I will always be obedient. It is if I submit; therefore, I am. I am what? I am obedient now, for the moment. Submission is not a one-time event. If obedience is the reaction of submission, and since his Word and His voice comes to us continually, we need to be obedient continually, we need to choose continually. We must, therefore, submit continually. When I submit, I am in obedience at that moment. Therefore, if I submit, I am. It is not if I submit, I will always be. Therefore, let us continue in submission. Submit and obey.

Do I want my enemies to be His enemies?

Do I want my adversaries to be His adversaries?

Do I want to come out of my wilderness in power, anointed, to be sent?

Submit and Obey.

VI. Receive Authority from the Father – In a later chapter, we will discover that the wilderness is where Jesus received the Father's authority. Jesus could not go into ministry immediately after the river baptism experiences because He did not yet have the Father's authority.

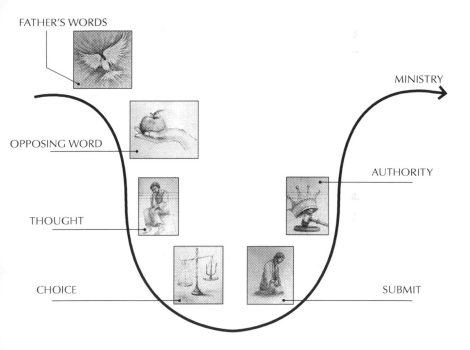

FATHER'S WORDS

OPPOSING WORD

THOUGHT

CHOICE

MINISTRY

AUTHORITY

SUBMIT

VII. Engage-Once authority is received, we now are positioned to place the Father's authority into action, to engage Satan. We go on the attack! The result is power. Like Jesus, we can exhibit the Holy Spirit's power just before coming out of the wilderness as well.

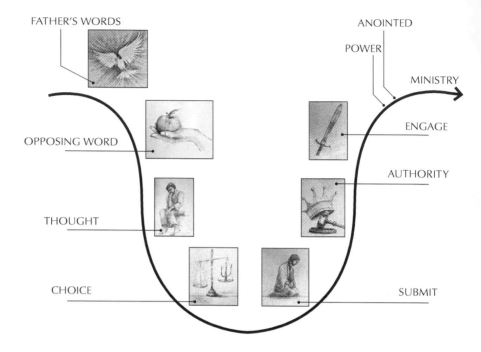

FATHER'S WORDS

ANOINTED

POWER

MINISTRY

OPPOSING WORD

ENGAGE

AUTHORITY

THOUGHT

CHOICE

SUBMIT

Scripture shows us that Jesus went through these seven separate steps in His wilderness walk. Each one was unique. Before he could move on to the next, He needed to experience the previous one. Each offered a specific opportunity. All combined, they enabled Jesus to maneuver himself away from the torment Satan had for Him, ultimately allowing himself to be free of Satan's influence, allowing Him to walk out and sent by the Father into ministry.

We can see that Jesus resisted the devil by speaking the Word of God to Satan in the wilderness. We can also see that Satan fled from Jesus in the wilderness. He could not stay. Witnessing this process, we can also understand that Satan exited the wilderness, unable to influence Jesus. With Satan's exit, we can see that Jesus resisted and how Jesus resisted. In like manner, we can see that Jesus had to submit. By taking Jesus' example, we must also submit to the Lord, then resist, and Satan will flee. Having received the Father's authority and placing it into action, the result is the power of the Holy Spirit. When action is applied, power is the result. We simply need to walk our talk. The process was there for Jesus. The process is also there for you and me in our wilderness walk. We now have a road map. Satan must leave your wilderness too!

CHAPTER 9

The Need, The Opportunity, Fulfillment in Relevancy

Where are we in history today? The gay lifestyle is normalized. Abortion is the world's answer as a medical solution to conception, a holy event. States are running legal numbers games. Pornography is rampant. Many of our children do not know what gender they are. Addictions are at an epidemic level. Recently euthanasia has been suggested on the political stump. There is huge unrest that is dividing our country. A pandemic is upon us. Daily, headlines amaze with concepts rooted in arrogance, malice, and other ungodly characteristics. Darkness has challenged morality in our country with a degree of success.

Several years ago, in the news headlines, we heard that an Islamist militant group in Nigeria abducted more than 200 Nigerian schoolgirls. There were reports that the group threatened to sell them into slavery. News reported crucifixions with others having their heads cut off for political and religious reasons. There were two crucifixions in eastern Syria, and 23 others executed. *History.com,* updated: June 07, 2019, Original July 10, 2017 prints, "ISIS fighters attacked a northern town in Iraq that was home to the Yazidis, a minority religious group, in August 2014. They killed hundreds of people, sold women into slavery, forced religious conversions, and caused tens of thousands of Yazidis to flee from their homes." Understand that is what darkness wants of man. God made you in His image, but Satan wants you enslaved, or he wants you dead.

My son and his family visit us in the summer, staying at the shore nearby for about a week. One day while my wife and I visited them, our family put on our swimming suits and went to the beach. It was not long after our arrival that several little joyful faces took my hand and led me into the waves. Pappy had to go along. After swimming, body surfing, and general play in the water, Pappy got tired! I decided to stand and rest in the water about chest high and watched everyone enjoying themselves. Some were throwing the Frisbee. Others were playing in the water while many were sunbathing, chatting, or soaking in the sun on the sand. I noticed the noise level was significantly high, with my grandchildren contributing their share. Standing there in the water next to the beach, I saw the outgoing undercurrent washing sand from under my feet. Each wave would take a little more out to the ocean, and if I had not moved to reposition, I would have lost my balance and fallen.

In an instant, the thought occurred to me this scene was a picture of today. Pondering those thoughts, I understood. On the surface, we are enjoying ourselves in a general state of festivity, or worse, apathy. But underneath the surface, we are unaware that our moral and ethical foundation is eroding by currents in our society that are not of God. Without an adjustment, we will lose our stability and fall. That erosion is going on under the water line and threatening our stability given by the Father, Son, and Holy Spirit. The darkness is getting darker. Acceleration of darkness is rapidly advancing. The question, therefore, is this. What happens if the church does not get brighter? For many of us, our light has grown dull. That is not a condemnation but too often a reality, none the less. Why is that? Darkness through the world has lied to us. We, Christ's church, are exiles. Let us know that darkness has a definite agenda and a desired goal.

Pastor John Betts of Abundant Life Church in Georgetown, Delaware gave me the first opportunity to publicly share *Road Map Through the Wilderness* in his church. To determine if there would be enough interest in sharing at Wednesday night Bible studies, he invited me to speak on a Sunday morning. At the end of the message, he gave an altar call, an invitation for those who wanted prayer regarding the topic I shared, an overview *of Road Map Through the Wilderness.* Based on previous experiences in other churches, I expected him and several leaders of the church to join me, each ministering to individuals as they presented themselves. To my surprise, he nor anyone else joined me at the altar rail. Many lined up single file, down one aisle, waiting for me to pray individually with them. As each approached me, they would share why they were there, their wilderness experience, where they were hurting. In hearing their cry to the Lord, I was able to determine the intensity of their pain. Pastor Betts closed the service, considering the number of people still waiting and the length of time spent per person. All those still waiting for ministry, however, stayed in line. None left. Somehow this message touched a tender place of need in their heart deep where they were hurting. After I prayed with several people, I looked back, seeing that all in line sat down in the pews on either side of the aisle. They were all still waiting.

I noticed that all except one were gray-haired or graying. Everyone coming to the altar was in deep pain; some were in deep distress, some dismayed. It occurred to me that those individuals waiting and responding to this theme was the strength of this church. All were well-rooted and seasoned in the Lord. Although the Lord's thoughts are greater than our thoughts, I could not help but wonder if the Lord was revealing a silent but aggressive attack at the inner core, these individual leaders of His church. As the Lord has continued to allow me to share this word over the years, I see a similar pattern without exception. I cannot help but wonder if this is an event unfolding with seasoned Christians around the world? Is it a surgically focused, under the radar attack on lives in the body of Christ?

Does your light need to get brighter? Is it time to get yourself out of your wilderness walk? Do you need to come out of the wilderness in authentic power, ministered to and strengthened for kingdom work, strengthened for Holy Spirit battle in a world that is getting darker? Do you need to grasp discernment, not only for ministry anointing but for the practical needs in your life, in a world that is rapidly changing before your eyes? Only you can answer these questions for yourself. If not already clear in your mind, I pray the Lord will demonstrate them for you in these pages of *Road Map Through the Wilderness.*

Jesus' wilderness walk reveals that we have an opportunity to be released from Satan's influence in our wilderness experience, a truth I did not previously understand. I can now be the aggressor with the expectation that Satan will flee in my wilderness walk. By Jesus' example I can influence the one or ones who have devised the trials and temptations I experience there. I now recognize that I can be a threat to any spiritual influence that tries to affect my walk as a Christian negatively. I can impact spiritual opposition in my own life that will make the enemy turn and run. I now understand that my wilderness experience is an opportunity.

Now that I understand that truth, by using Jesus' example, by taking action, darkness will take notice. **Acts 19:15(NIV),** *"One day the evil spirit answered them, 'Jesus I know, and Paul I know about, but who are you?"* Os Hillman poses a question in *TGIF Today God Is First Volume 1, June 09, 2016,* by asking a simple question, "Are you a threat to the kingdom of darkness?" He asks how many of us sit in church every Sunday, posing little threat to Satan's dark kingdom when his mandate is to hinder anyone seeking an effective full walk with God. Can darkness approach you and ask, "who are you?" If your destiny is to conform to Jesus' image, you will also find yourself in conflict with the enemy as you become a threat. Know, however, that, *"greater is He that is in you, than he that is in the world"* **I John 4:4b (NKJV)**. Know that if you are in God's will, the enemy will try everything to hinder you. Mr. Hillman also points out that, "God permits temptation," that it, "drives us deeper into the soil of God." As we experience trials and temptations, he indicates that our Father has an agenda as well.

Isaiah 54:17(NASB), *'No weapon that is formed against you will prosper; and every tongue that accuses you in judgment you will condemn. This is the heritage of the servants of the LORD, AND their vindication is from Me, declares the LORD.'* This heritage is the will of our Lord in your life. Considering the impact darkness brings to our lives, how many of us need to do a better job presenting ourselves as opposed to a real, active, spiritual enemy? Understand there are remnants. There is a core of churches, of individuals, who are walking in anointing and power every day. They have already been sent, like Jesus. I know a young pastor in India, who, in one month, had eleven small crusades with one hundred eighty-five souls saved and baptized. He has seen many healings, deliverances, salvations, and baptisms in these events. What is your gift? Are you today walking in, *"the heritage of the servants of the Lord?* "Yes," you might say, "I am to some degree," but are we walking to the extent needed in this hour and the hour to come?

John 1:4(NASB), *"In Him was life, and the life was the light of men."* Again, an honest question to be asked is this. How much life is the light of the church giving to the Lord today? How much life am I giving the Lord today? I, for one, have room to improve.

These questions are certainly not a condemnation, but can this be a time for us to evaluate our walk with our Lord, Jesus? Christ's life illuminates from my light and your light. Since our Lord does not have a heart of condemnation, the issue is not, woe is me an unclean sinner. It is, how I can take advantage of the opportunity to enable sending, *"the rod of Your strength,"* His authority, to come, *"out of Zion,"* that's you and me, and *"rule in the midst of Your,"* Jesus', *"enemies"* **Psalm110:2(NKJV)**, Lord, allow our light to be brighter that we may walk in the power of the Holy Spirit, in His anointing, in dominion, thus, placing Jesus' enemies under His feet and thus giving Jesus, none other than the Messiah, life. Can you see your role in **Psalm 111:6(NASB)** that says, **"He has made known to His people the power of His works, in giving them the heritage of the nations."** Can you see who you are, your identity through your Father's eyes? Have you received the *"heritage of the nations?"* Are you walking in the *"power of His works,"* in whatever gifting you have? How can you do that? How can I walk in that heritage? Jesus, in the wilderness, has demonstrated those answers!

Steve Wingfield says in his book, *Winning the Race Every Day,* "You were raised to new life by trusting God's mighty power-the same power that raised Christ from the dead. That power now works in you. Ask yourself these questions: you trusted God's power to save you, but do you trust it to work in your life now? Are you expecting God's powerful works as you walk with him? God has a power that can create universes and raise people from the dead! Thank God today for your life. Watch for His mighty power at work in you and give him the glory as you tell the story of your new life."

Are we batting 1000? Jesus says if we have the faith of a mustard seed, we can move mountains. Do you need to move a mountain? Possibly a more appropriate question is, are you prepared to move it?

Mr. Os Hillman asks this question. "Are You Becoming Secularized?"

TGIF Today God Is First Volume 2 by Os Hillman, Wednesday, May 11, 2016

"Therefore, God gave them over in the sinful desires of their hearts to sexual impurity for the degrading of their bodies with one another. They exchanged the truth of God for a lie and worshiped and served created things rather than the Creator-who is forever praised. Amen" **(Rom 1:24- 25 NIV).**

Mr. Hillman tells a familiar story about a frog in a kettle. When one places a frog in a warm water kettle, it does not notice that the water temperature was getting hotter gradually until it is too late. It eventually dies from the heat, not realizing the danger it had. Mr. Hillman says, "Societies are suffering from the "frog in the kettle" analogy. They make decisions that seem innocent enough to realize the impact these decisions bring to their society later." Our country now stands on the edge of collapse if we allow socialism in our government and open our country's borders. Let us consider that Christianity will be on the verge of attack if we enable a government to overshadow the system our forefathers have given us. These will allow spiritual influences in our country to embrace behavior that history has already proven fatal for a country that chooses it. Mr. Hillman says, "whether the issue is gay rights, abortion, euthanasia, or simply a lack of spiritual influence over society, the changes seem logical to the unregenerate mind but reveal the nation's moral compass of the nation has been removed."

He speaks of *Towards the Conversion of England*, a book written in 1945, produced by the Church of England Commission on Evangelism, chaired by the evangelical Bishop of Rochester, Christopher Chavasse. It is about the spiritual scenario in England at that time. It states that thirty percent of the English population attended church then. Today, church attendance is in the single digits. "England is no longer a Christian nation," it says.

We see similar results in America now. The number attending church is declining, and the vision our forefathers had when they created America is rapidly deteriorating. *Towards the Conversion of England"* (1945 states), "The reason is that more and more believers are seeing the local church as irrelevant to the world they live in." It continues saying that it is not a question of them teaching the Bible; it is a question of making it **relevant** to their world.

It is relevancy! Do you need relevancy in your life? Do you desire to receive, demonstrate, and implement relevancy today with identity, authority, power, anointing, all to be sent just like Jesus? That is the walk that will make you fulfilled. In *Road Map Through the Wilderness,* and the second series, *It is Finished but Not Yet Complete*, we will learn to come out of the wilderness and, "rule in the midst of His enemies!" Fulfill in me, Lord, that which you have created me to be. I desire to be relevant today.

"The brother of humble circumstances is to glory his high position."

Isaiah 54:17b(NASB).
TGIF Today God Is First by Os Hillman

"Whenever God takes a saint to a very lowly state, it is designed to accomplish something only that process can do. *"He reveals the deep things of darkness and brings deep shadows into the light"* **Job 12:22(NET Bible).**" He explains that Job's trials allowed him to learn things about God, himself, and his friends that we all needed to know. "God reveals things in the dark places of circumstances that He will use to show something

He wants you and others to know." Mr. Hillman makes a good point that the Lord uses our wilderness experiences to prepare us for His work in, "high positions." It is in the wilderness where we learn the things of God, where we make our decisions regarding God. Is God preparing you for a high position? Is God preparing you for that which He has created you to be? Let us surely see this wilderness is placing us in a high position by our Lord. It positions us to come out with an opportunity to be sent into anointed ministry. It allows us to make a difference, just like Jesus. It is an opportunity to be fulfilled in Him so that your life is generating His life. It is an opportunity to be relevant in the kingdom of God and the lives of humans.

CHAPTER 10

That Small Two-Letter Word

Satan's tactics resemble a temptation used in my childhood by playmates. Of course, I never did this, but I know someone who did, I say with a mischievous wink. The temptation is the dare. "Go ahead," we would say, "I dare you to jump over that wide ditch. You cannot do that. Prove to me that you can." And the temptation to bring potential harm to yourself is given, something that exposes risk. And of course, the dreaded double dare challenge is given if the child does not yield and jump. Everyone knew that meant you had to jump. Precisely, that is what Satan was doing to Jesus. He was challenging Jesus' identity as the Son of God. The challenge is not without danger. The risk was losing all that Jesus had available to Him as Son of God. And it all was done by using that little word "*if.*"

We see in **Luke 4:3(NKJV)**, discussed earlier, the word "if" is, used. *"And the devil said to Him, if you are the Son of God, command this stone to become bread."* In **Luke 4:5-7(NKJV)**, the Bible says, *"Then the devil, taking Him up on a high mountain, showed Him all the kingdoms of the world in a moment of time. And the devil said to Him, "All this authority I will give You, and their glory; for this has been delivered to me, and I give it to* *whomever I wish. Therefore, if You will worship before me, all will be Yours.*" We also see **Luke 4:9(AMPC)**, saying, "*Then he took Him to Jerusalem and set Him on [f]a gable of the temple, and said to Him, if You are the Son of God, cast Yourself down from here.*" It is no coincidence that Satan used the same little word in each of his three temptations. Satan is questioning Jesus' identity in His mind as the Son of God. He is trying to get Jesus to think about it, understanding that if Jesus does so, He might doubt. If Jesus doubts, Satan just might change Jesus' mind about His identity. It is subtle, but it is there. It was at the riverbank where the Father told Jesus He was His Son. He heard with His natural ears and processed that with His mind, but Jesus had to make His own decision for Himself. God is a gentleman. He did not force His identity on Jesus. The Father allowed Jesus to make His own decision. He did it in the wilderness.

Nor will He force His identity on you. He allows you to choose for yourself as well. It is the wilderness, in those difficult and trying times, where we choose who we are, our identity, as a son or daughter of the Father or a brother or sister of the Messiah. Our wilderness walk is the same process Jesus faced. God puts our identity in place first by speaking His Word to us. We hear the Word of salvation spoken from the pulpit, from an acquaintance, and perhaps on television as the spoken Word. Or we discover it in the Bible, the written Word. In our invitation to invite Jesus in our lives, the Lord places our identity as a son/daughter in heaven. Thus, the Holy Spirit will lead us into the wilderness with Satan arriving with an opposing word, always something contrary to what the Father says, to get us to doubt or question our identity that the Father's Word gives us.

Many years ago, my wife and I attended a retreat in Williamsburg, Virginia, hosted by evangelist Earl Tyson. One day, an attendee shared a story that illustrates Satan's tactic in his attempt to sway Jesus. Based on personal experiences, I believe it to be an accurate demonstration, although not explicitly referenced in the Bible. The story explains that Satan is standing with a very tiny box in the palm of his hand. In the box was his greatest weapon. One would wonder what could be so powerful but be so small. The box revealed a tiny wedge when opened.

I burn wood as my primary source of heat in my house. I find myself splitting large pieces of oak and wild cherry wood with a wedge. When I strategically place a wedge in a crack, even the biggest pieces will slowly break and ultimately fall into two parts as I consistently apply pressure with a maul. Even the most stubborn pieces will eventually split with the wedge placed at precisely the right spot, a spot where there is weakness.

In challenging Jesus, Satan was trying to find a little crack in His identity, placing a wedge of doubt in Jesus' mind, trying to break His most significant identity as Son. It would be fair to say the pressure applied was in the form of constant temptation for forty days. It was a focused attempt to create a crack in the identity the Father confirmed in Jesus at the riverbank. Satan will try to change your identity as a son or daughter of God as well. Let us be careful not to provide him a sure opportunity for exploiting doubt by allowing him to create a small crack in our identity.

If Jesus's presence on earth so threatens Satan, why wouldn't he try to take Jesus's life? Why wouldn't Satan try to attack Jesus physically? Why wouldn't he try to overtake Jesus by power instead of temptation? After all, Jesus is human. Wouldn't that be the logical method Satan would use? The answer is in this question. Mothers, how might you react if someone came to destroy your child? Would it be an understatement to say you would be more than upset? If someone threatened the very life of that child, wouldn't you fight with reckless abandon? Why would Satan want to change Jesus' identity as Son rather than kill Him? **Isaiah 14:11-12(NKJV)**, *"Your pomp is brought down to Sheol and the sound of your stringed instruments: the maggot is spread under* *you. And worms cover you. How you are fallen from Heaven, O Lucifer, son of the morning? How are you cut to the ground, you who weakened the nation's?"* If Satan tried to overcome Jesus with aggression, he knew that he would upset Father God. Satan had already experienced and lost one battle when the Father threw him out of heaven. He does not want to experience that degradation again. Satan knows he cannot reckon with the power of the Father. Already having experienced the wrath of the Father once, Satan knows he would lose. Satan is afraid. FEAR of the Father is what kept him from harming Jesus bodily.

Of Job, God said to Satan, *"do not lay a hand on this person"* **Job 1:12b(NKJV)**. Satan could not touch Job's physical body. Could it be that the Father was also displaying this same principle with Jesus? Why does Satan not try to overtake you and me by personal physical aggression? He cannot just overpower us physically unless we give him the authority to do that. Could it be because you also are an authentic child of God made in His image, just like Job? Satan will not lay a hand on you because the Father says of you too, *"do not lay a hand on this person."* Satan's only recourse is to change Jesus' identity. I will not harm Him, is Satan's attitude toward Jesus' physical person. Satan's actions demonstrate that he is attempting to change Jesus' understanding of who He is as Son of God. The result would be the same if Satan personally attacked Jesus, even if he killed Him. Jesus' identity as Son would be negated, whether by physical death or by changing His identity in the Father, which is spiritual death, either way. If Jesus no longer thought of Himself as the Son of God, He would not be able to fulfill **I John 3:8b**, *"For this purpose the Son of God was manifested, that He might destroy the works of the devil."* Jesus cannot destroy the works of the devil if He chooses Satan. As a child of God, Satan's actions demonstrate that he is attempting to change an understanding of who you are as well. If you choose Satan in the wilderness, it will negate your identity as a son or daughter. If you yield to Satan's temptations, you will no longer be able to respond as God's son/daughter.

What does the Father say of you in the wilderness? Just like Job, "do not lay a hand on this person." Let us not underestimate His authority, power, and love applied to you. There is an identity to grab hold of; the Father's identity of you as son or daughter! Our identity of self in God's eyes is necessary to walk a victorious Christian life. It is also crucial for us to understand our identity as Jesus' brother/sister and the Father's son/daughter when we are in the wilderness.

Another question screams for us to answer. How does the Father see us, His church? God does not look at your past or present to determine who you are, your identity. We can see that demonstrated in Gideon. **Judges 6:12(AMPC)**, *"And the Angel of the Lord appeared to him and said to Him, The Lord is with you, you mighty man of [fearless] courage."* That is quite an endorsement! This man, Gideon, must be somebody important in the kingdom. Could he be the Lord's champion leading many regiments, winning many battles? Then in **Judges 6:14(AMPC)**, *"The Lord turned to him and said, "Go in this your' might, and you shall save Israel from the hand of Midian. Have I not sent you?".*

Even Jesus recognizes Gideon as a man of might and with courage. He is sending Gideon to save the whole nation of Israel. Gideon's response, however, in **Judges 6:15(AMPC)** illuminates quite another identity. *"Gideon said to Him, "Oh Lord, how can I deliver Israel? Behold, my clan is the poorest in Manasseh, and I am the least in my father's house."* Gideon sees himself as the lowest of the lowest. In his wildest imagination, he cannot envision himself as a leader who will save Israel. In **Judges 6:16(AMPC)** the Lord responds, *"Surely I will be with you, and you shall smite the Midianites as one man."* We tend to think if I do, then I am, or, if I do, I will be, or who I am in the world is who I am in the Kingdom of God. Your identity in the world does not matter. It does not matter who the world perceives you to be. What matters is who God has created you to be. It is to conform to the image of Christ, which opens a myriad of possibilities. **Romans 8:29(NKJV)**, *"For whom He foreknew, He also predestined to conform to the image of His Son."* With Gideon, the Lord says you already are, so now you choose and walk in it. In **Romans 4:17(NKJV)** God, *"calls into being that which does not exist."* Since God already knows who He created you to be, it is your choice to come into alignment with that, just like Jesus did.

We can see in Gideon's response that the Lord called a mighty warrior identity into him, which he did not acknowledge. **Romans 8:14(NKJV)**, *"For as many as are led by the Spirit of God, these are the sons of God."* Choose to be led by God! He has already given you identity in Him. **Jeremiah 29:11(NKJV)**, *"For I know the thoughts that I think toward you, says the Lord, thoughts of peace and not of evil, to give you a future and a hope."* He created you for a purpose. May the Lord fulfill in you that which He has created you to be. **II Corinthians 5:15(NIV)**, *"And He died for all, that those who live should no longer live for themselves but for Him who died for them and was raised again."* It is the Lord's view of us that counts.

Poor Me

Observation of Jesus' choices in the wilderness and resulting response to Satan brings us to predictable solutions in our own wilderness experiences. To give us more vision, I would ask you this question. What was the character of Jesus' response to Satan in the wilderness? One class attendee jokingly said, "I do not understand the question, so how can I give you an answer?"

Let us explore the character in which Jesus did not respond. We can agree Jesus' response to Satan was not "Oh Father; big bad Satan is causing such problems for me. He is confusing me about your Word and taunting me to do things that I should not do. His offers are so tempting, and I do not know what to do. Please help me, Father? Please tell me what I should do?" These responses certainly are not an accurate characterization of Jesus' response to Satan. Jesus did not play the role of the victim!

Mike Murdock says in his daily *Morning Motivation*, "Any wounded animal attracts attack. Weakness is an invitation to bullies. Don't talk nor think like a victim of your circumstances. You are more than a conqueror. Act like it. Talk like it. The love of God is keeping you today." **Romans 8: 35, 37(KJV)**, *"Who shall separate us from the love of Christ? Shall tribulation, or distress,* *or persecution, or famine, or nakedness, or peril, or sword? Ney, in all these things we are more than conquerors through Him that loved us."* Indeed, Jesus was not a victim. He did not plead, feel sorry for himself, or display any attributes other than being an aggressor in His most challenging wilderness experiences.

I can undoubtedly say that how I envisioned myself, especially in my wilderness experiences, did not coincide with the identity the Father has of me. I certainly was not an aggressor but resembled a victim. Observing many others, I have seen people esteem themselves lower than the Lord's opinion. Many people struggle to the point of depression, even resulting in suicide because they are overly critical or have a wrong understanding of who they are and who their true identity in the Lord is.

Many years ago, a church in Richmond, Virginia, invited my wife and me to share music. Several weeks prior, Donna had been contemplating thoughts about the image we hold of ourselves, mainly focused on a female perspective. During the trip, she was impressed to organize her thoughts on paper. By the time we completed the drive, she had everything organized. When we arrived in time for Sunday school classes, they asked if we wanted to share with the adult Sunday school class. Unprepared, we looked at each other with surprise. The obvious choice was for her to unfold her thoughts that she prepared just hours earlier. Her presentation lasted for most of the hour allowed, with the class ending just in time for worship service. The next several minutes presented a most unusual response that neither of us could have anticipated. She was immediately surrounded by many of the ladies, all asking questions for additional information and clarification. The topic of her discussion, how they perceived themselves, resulted in a remarkable response that ministered to an obvious need touching a tender place in their spirit. My observation was that nearly all were struggling with their image, their perception of their worth. Their opinion of themselves can be described no other way except low esteem. How do you see yourself compared to how the Lord sees you? Applicable to our topic here, having an incorrect understanding of our identity, of low esteem, do we respond in our wilderness scenario as victims? Do we have a low opinion of our worth, ultimately falling into an attitude of pity?

For many years, Donna and I attended as many services as possible when Evangelist Earl Tyson visited the area. Eventually, we sat on his board of directors and were personally very close to him. Occasionally, Earl would arrive in our area unannounced from time to time. On one occasion, a friend invited us to attend a spur of the moment potluck dinner, with about ten other couples attending. Arriving at the host home, Earl met us just outside the house with his huge smile and arms held wide. As he greeted me, he asked, "How are you today?" At that time, I was suffering from a tragedy in my life. So there, on the screened-in porch, I proceeded to tell him every detail. After my lengthy response, spiritual bleeding, which he was not expecting, we went into the house, ate our dinner, and had fellowship with our friends for a time afterward.

The fellowship was interrupted when the host asked Earl if he had anything to share for the evening. Without hesitation, he began speaking on what he called The Poor Me Syndrome. It did not take long for me to determine he was talking about me, to me. We had previously looked at Gideon in **Judges 6** and discovered that people see themselves based on where they are in their circumstances at any given moment and that God sees a person based on who our Lord created us to be.

Gideon also demonstrates the Poor Me Syndrome quite well. **Judges 6:12(AMPC)**, *"and the angel of the Lord appeared to him and said to him, the Lord is with you, mighty man of [fearless] courage. And Gideon said to him, O sir, if the Lord is with us, why is all this befallen us? And where are all his wondrous works of which our fathers told us, saying, did not the Lord bring us up* *from Egypt? But now the Lord has forsaken us and given us into the hand of Midian."* And there it is, The Poor Me Syndrome. He is personalizing himself as poor Gideon. *"The Lord turned to him and said, 'Go in this your might, and you shall save Israel from the hand of Midian. Have I not sent you? Gideon said to him, Oh Lord, how can I deliver Israel? Behold, my clan is the poorest in Manasseh, and I am the least in my Father's house."* We see it again. Gideon is arguing with the Lord, trying to convince Him he cannot complete what the Lord created him to do, what the Lord was instructing him to do at that moment because of his self-perceived lowly status. He was feeling sorry for himself. *"The Lord said to him, "Surely, I will be with you, and you shall smite the Midianites as one man."* He was pleading with Gideon.

Gideon doubts his identity in the Lord because he is a victim of the circumstances that he finds himself in the world. Too many times in my difficulties, I displayed the same victim identity, the Poor Me Spirit. Too often, my quickness to identify as a victim became fertile ground for Satan's agenda, bringing on despair, fear, anxiety, anger, and other fruits of darkness resulting from victim identity. He would have us display behavior and attitudes inappropriate for a child of God. Satan's agenda is to have us display behavior from perspectives, ultimately leading us to the point of unbelief.

Lord, use these trials and temptations to illuminate the inappropriate characteristics I show in my wilderness struggles. Lord, help me to receive an understanding so I might ask forgiveness for harboring them. Establish my identity in You to form in my spirit, a righteous identity. Establish an identity appropriate for a child of God and a citizen of the Kingdom of Heaven. Cleanse me of influences within that would birth those behaviors and attitudes. Help me walk in holiness and come out of the wilderness in authentic power, the power of the Holy Spirit brought forth by a correct understanding of who I am in You. Amen!

CHAPTER 12

Limitations Based on Expectations

We can understand much as we look at the heart of our Lord in **II Kings 4:1-6(AMPC)**, *"Now the wife of a son of the prophets cried to Elisha, your servant my husband is dead, and you know that your servant feared the Lord. But the creditor has come to take my two sons to be his slaves. Elisha said to her, 'What shall I do for you? Tell me, what have you [of sale value] in the house'? She said, 'Your handmaid has nothing in the house except a jar of oil.' Then he said, 'Go around and borrow vessels from all your neighbors, empty vessels—and not a few.' And when you come in, shut the door upon you and your sons. Then pour out [the oil you have] into all those vessels, setting aside each one when it is full. So she went from him and shut the door upon herself and her sons, who brought to her the vessels as she poured the oil. When the vessels were all full, she said to her son, bring me another vessel. And he said to her, there is not a one left. Then the oil stopped multiplying."*

Elisha was the leader of the prophets in that day. The recent death of one of his prophets caused this scenario to unfold. In those days, the sons were responsible for the debt of their father. The widow found herself in a significant wilderness experience. She lost her spouse and her two sons were to be taken away by the creditors to work off their father's debt. They will not be able to provide for her. She has lost her whole family and her income.

In response to her dilemma, it is interesting to note that Elisha did not offer to help her financially in his response, to give her money. He did not go to the other prophets and take a collection. His assistance unfolded in a very different way. He focused on the one item she had of value, the oil, and it miraculously multiplied. It multiplied as she poured from the full vessel to the empty ones.

Of significance, here is what the Lord illustrates in verse **II Kings 4:6(AMPC)**, " *When the vessels were all full, she said to her son, Bring me another vessel. And he said to her, There is not a one left. Then the oil stopped multiplying.*" If it were me in this situation, and if I knew in advance that the oil would only stop flowing when the jars were full, I would have moved all the furniture outside and filled the floor with empty vessels(jars). And knowing that, I would have asked the boys to build shelves on the walls and fill them with even more jars. Also, knowing that truth in advance, I would have had the boys hang shelves from the ceiling and fill them with vessels. I would have brought many more jars for the Lord to fill because it was only when the jars were full that the oil stopped flowing. As we can see, she did not have this information in advance. In this illustration, we see the Lord blessing in multiplied proportions until all the vessels were full. Let us understand the basis for the widow's significant blessing was the number of jars she chose to borrow. We can see the number of vessels the widow borrowed was dependent on her interpretation of how much the Lord wanted to bless her. Elisha did not give her a specific number of jars to borrow. He just said to get, "*not a few*" **II Kings 4:3b(AMPC)**. Therefore, the blessing the widow received from the Lord was determined by the number of jars she received from her neighbors. The number of vessels she received from her neighbors was determined by her expectation of what she thought the Lord would provide. The oil stopped flowing when the vessels were full. She could have had more oil if she had brought in more jars. In other words, the basis of her limitations was her limited expectations of how much the Lord would bless her.

A similar miracle unfolded when Jesus fed the 5,000. The disciples wanted to go into town and buy food for all, but Jesus chose a very different method. When He blessed the few loaves and fishes provided by a young boy, they were multiplied and fed the crowd with twelve baskets left over.

Many years ago, I had a need when a significant financial issue developed in my business. The loss was substantial! The problem carried with it the possibility of liquidation, of losing my business completely. The exposure not only threatened my ability to make a living but to liquidate would bring a loss of pennies on the dollar to the value of the business. Looking at all options, I considered working in the industry but changing focus to another area entirely.

Changing careers was even a possibility. Not knowing what to do, I turned to the Lord, who led me to this scripture, **II Kings 4**. After prayer, applying this scripture to the business, understanding the Lord blessed what the widow already had, I asked the Lord to bless what I already had. To generate new business activity, I looked through my clientele list for potential business. Immediately several possibilities became apparent that I had not considered before. Prospecting activity led to sales, and sales led to income. Over time, the financial crisis changed from critical to significant, then from significant to neutral, and ultimately from neutral to thriving. The Lord multiplied what I already had. Understand, our God is a God of multiplication, and in each of these incidents, he multiplied an asset that was previously available. Selah! We see Satan, on the other hand, can only function in subtraction and division. Understanding this truth, we can recognize him in our lives by these fruits.

I shudder to think all I have missed in life because I have placed my limitations on the blessings I expected from our Lord. His heart is to bless. **John 10:10(NKJV)**, *"I have come that they might have life and that they may have it more abundantly."* Now in the late autumn of my life, it is my earnest prayer that these words the Lord is sharing with us will illuminate an understanding to all a better understanding of His heart. He wants you to be blessed!

II Kings 4:7(AMPC), *"Then she came and told the man of God. He said, "Go, sell your oil, and pay your debt, and you and your sons live on the rest."* Here lies the magnificence of our Lord. The miracle was the multiplied jar of oil. The blessings were that she was able to pay the debt. Elimination of debt also released her boys from servitude, and the Lord provided her a retirement plan as well. In her wilderness situation, she found her blessing. Let us understand that our wilderness experiences may also be the stage for blessings. Our God is a God of restoration. Our God is a God of multiplication. The widow presented the need to Elisha. Elisha heard the Father's voice. The Lord used Elisha as His voice. The widow and the boys obeyed. Grace, unmerited favor, provided for the need, and the Lord multiplied the oil. Can anyone say, "Praise the Lord?"

God introduced a fascinating scenario that I did not first see when I read it.

One day I chose to follow Elisha's instructions to the widow and apply them in my local neighborhood. I planned to ask neighbors to borrow their pots and pans, and get, *"not a few"* **II Kings 4:3b(AMPC)**. It would have been an easy exercise to implement, except for one detail. The neighbors probably would ask why I wanted to empty their cabinets, especially those neighbors I did not know. My hesitation in doing so was that I realized I would have had to humble myself, embarrass myself by answering their question with the words, "The Lord told me to do it." Would I have had the courage to do so, I would not be embarrassing myself now, admitting that I chose not to implement this project. Unfortunately, humility is what I now experience, sharing this with you, humility then, or humility now? Looking back, I would have preferred then. Regardless, it was a humiliating experience for me. As for the widow and her boys, we cannot determine why humility would have a good practice for them, but none the less, they chose to follow Elijah's instructions. And the result was a great blessing. Selah!

CHAPTER 13

Fulfill What You Have Been Created to Be

Jack Hayford, in his devotional book *Praise in the Presence of God,* says, "The instant you receive Jesus as your Savior, you entered a new standing with God. The epistle to the Romans repeatedly uses the word justified to describe this action. It is a giant of a concept – a word meaning that God, the judge of all humankind, has made a legal judgment about you and me. When we trust in Christ, He not only declares us holy, He also gives his legal reasons for doing so. Because we are putting our trust in the righteousness of Christ, God puts the sinless record of Jesus as a credit to our account. He not only removes this record of our guilt but also enters the record of Christ's absolute sinlessness! And we are born again, a new birth." Why is it important that He enters the record of Christ's absolute sinlessness? It is because we get to start anew with a new identity.

Romans 8:29(NIV), "*For those God foreknew.*" **Psalm139:16 (NKJV)**, "*Your eyes saw my substance, being yet unformed. And in Your book they all were written, The days fashioned for me, When as yet there were none of them.*" Who is He referencing here? He foreknew you and me. The Lord knew us in our mother's womb. He also planned for you to conform to the image of Jesus. Since it is your destiny, choose to be led by God. He has already given you an identity. That is, who you already are in His mind. Do not choose the identity based on the choices you make in the world. Do not choose the identity the world tries to place on you. Do not choose the identity of the outward man or woman the world has thrust upon you. That is not who you are! Choose the identity the Father has given you. Why? It enables you to come out of your wilderness. It is also because you, too, can be sent like Jesus. For what purpose did Jesus come to earth? Remember **I John 3: 8b(NKJV)**, *"For this purpose the Son of God was manifested, that He might destroy the works of the devil."* Because of Jesus and the Holy Spirit, who is now in you, Satan becomes threatened. Conforming now to the image of Christ, he is afraid of you too! Therefore, Satan wants to render you ineffective to the cause of Jesus. When you invite Jesus into your life and receive His identity, you are born again. Being born again, you receive a birthright into the kingdom. Immediately you are predestined to conform to the image of Jesus.

Understand, when you invite the Lord into your life and receive *His* identity, you immediately receive a bull's eye on your chest, just like Jesus. That is because of **I John 3:8b.** Through Jesus, Satan sees us as having a common goal with our Lord to destroy his works. You can also expect to be led into a wilderness scenario because it is in the wilderness that you make your choice. The choice you make regarding Jesus determines your identity. The choice you make about your identity in Christ determines your actions. It is your actions in Jesus that concern Satan. Because of this, do you think Satan might try to place doubt in your mind as well? Do you believe Satan might try to get you to question your identity too? Do you think Satan might try to get into your head, try to engage a thought process, and try to influence you to his desired response? Of course, he will. **I Peter 4:12(NKJV),** *"Brother, do not think it strange concerning the fiery trial, which is to try you, as some strange thing happened to you."* It will be in our wilderness, in our dry place, a place where we are uncomfortable when we are weak. The wilderness is the time that the attack will come upon us. However, the good news is that our Lord, in this book, will demonstrate precisely how to counteract Satan's attempts and transfer his actions into activities of futility.

CHAPTER 14

I've Got the Advantage.

I Peter 1:6(NKJV), *"In this you greatly rejoice, though now for a little while, if need be, you have been grieved by various trials."* The Amplified Bible adds, *"and temptations."* I know of only one person who has never had a wilderness experience. She is a little old lady who dedicated herself to God many years ago. As a young woman, she chose to become a nun. Just before taking her permanent vows, she met a young man and fell in love. After a short time, she chose the young man, married, and lived a most fulfilling life, still walking in a deep commitment to the Lord. Not long ago, her husband passed on.

As I shared with her, introducing *Road Map Through the Wilderness*, she commented with a puzzled look, "I have never had a wilderness experience." It is not surprising to me as she is most humble, a most committed person, having one of the purest spirits I know. Taking on the teachings of her church, she is committed to a life of poverty, sacrificing all, mindful always of others, in prayer with fervor daily, and serving others when the opportunity arises. She lives an anointed life of servanthood. The Word above says, " *if need be, you have been grieved by various trials*." The Lord feels she does not need it. She does not need a wilderness experience to fulfill who the Lord created her to be.

The good news for us is if we need a wilderness walk, the Lord will orchestrate it for us; the Lord knows we are there. By Jesus giving the seven steps listed earlier, you can now see and understand where exactly you are in your wilderness, taking Jesus' example and move out. You can now be ready and prepared! Having the opportunity to expect Satan to arrive, you can look at this, our Father's Word, to show you how to maneuver through the wilderness. The good news now is that we are aware of the enemy's presence, which is the first step in defeating him. We now have confirmation that the Lord knows we are in the wilderness with Him, and most can expect it. By this, we have the advantage! **John 16:33(NASB)**, *"These things I have spoken to you, so that in Me you may have peace. In the world, you have tribulation but take courage; I have overcome the world."* Because Jesus is an overcomer, by His example, we can be overcomers too. Jesus walked down this road in the wilderness. By His example, He shows us what to do about our wilderness walk. He has given us a *Road Map*. Now I have the advantage.

Have you placed your identity as a brother or sister of Christ, not only understanding identity intellectually but also understanding it in your inner core? Have you received your identity by hearing the Father's Word, like Jesus on the riverbank giving opportunity for identity by personal choice in a difficult place? You are a threat too! Therefore, Satan is invested in your demise, as well! Do not let him intimidate you. It is not a coincidence that you are in a wilderness experience! Choose your identity as a son/daughter. Choose identity as a brother/sister. Satan has an agenda for you, but the Father says, you have a choice. Do not be discouraged. Now we can understand the Lord, in addition to Satan, has His agenda too. He shows us what that is in His *Road Map Through the Wilderness.*

Father, let me understand the significance of who I am in Jesus, that it is my destiny to conform to His image, and that I have the advantage, and I too am a threat to the enemy. Please help me understand you are showing me a process of hearing your voice, opposition, giving thought, making a choice, submitting, receiving authority, and placing into action the identity I choose. I choose Jesus. I choose you. I choose the Holy Spirit. Please help me to conform to that image. Amen

CHAPTER 15

Led Astray

We have learned what Satan did in the wilderness. That is temptations and trials. We have learned why he approached Jesus in the desert. It is because Jesus' arrival on earth threatened Satan. We have yet to determine how he tried to eliminate Jesus' own identity as the Son of God. It is a crucial point for us to understand this for a successful walk through our wilderness experience.

Romans 3:23(NKJV), "*for all have sinned and fall short of the glory of God.*" Every newborn baby is born into that truth. Nobody has to teach a young child how to lie. We are all born into the Adamic nature, the sin nature. Ultimately, we all need to choose the life we live, whether to continue walking in that sinful nature or to walk in a life with Christ as Lord. The Holy Spirit will be sharing with us how to go forward, not to fall short of God's glory, but how to be victorious in the struggles with Satan, particularly in our wilderness experience.

Hebrews 3: 7(NIV), "*So, as the Holy Spirit says,*" When I first read this verse, I understood these words only to mean what I was about to hear was authentic, that it was legitimate. Because the Holy Spirit said it, therefore, I considered it authentic. Consequently, I can be confident that it is true. Several years later, the Lord reminded me, the Holy Spirit led Jesus into the wilderness. He was there, present throughout Jesus' forty-day wilderness walk. By reading the events in **Hebrews 3**, we can see the Jewish people navigating their wilderness walk with the Holy Spirit present as well. Looking at their experiences, we can observe the parallels between their walk and Jesus' walk in the wilderness, revealing an understanding of our own wilderness experiences.

First, in **Hebrews 3**, we can see the Holy Spirit speaking in the first person revealing His presence in the wilderness walk of the Jewish people. However, it is essential that by His words, we see that He is not only present but also involved. Being involved, He might have first-hand information about Satan's ultimate objective for the Jewish people, and His purpose for Jesus in the wilderness as well. He knows these objectives, not only because He is part of the triune God, that is His omnipotence, but He was there as a personal observer commenting on the events. He understood precisely how the devil tried to change Jesus' identity because He was with Him. He was also with the Jewish nation in their wilderness walk. It is, in fact, He who is present in both events. The wilderness is important to Him. Take comfort in knowing that He is present with you in your wilderness trials and temptations as well.

Hebrews 3:8(NIV), *"Do not harden your hearts . . ."* Hardened are the hearts of the Jewish nation in their trek through the natural wilderness/desert. We can see those hardened hearts by their choices in the trials and temptations that the harsh wilderness exposed to them. This verse continues by comparing their actions, *". . . as you did in the rebellion"* **Hebrews 3:8(NIV)**. This rebellion in the wilderness was not the first time they rebelled. The Holy Spirit continues saying, *"during the time of testing in the wilderness"* **Hebrews 3:8(NIV)**. Know our wilderness walk is a time of trial for us as well. It is here that we have the opportunity to demonstrate our commitment to our Lord. Let us look at the Jewish wilderness walk observing their responses to trials and temptations. Then we can understand that our wilderness walk is challenging as well, allowing us to consider and avoid the same choices they made and the same consequences they experienced.

Hebrews 3:9(NKJV) demonstrates an interesting change in the Holy Spirit's commentary as He shares His thoughts, responding to the Jewish nation's sin. He says, ". . . *where your fathers tested Me, tried Me.*" We see the Holy Spirit now personally involved as He finds Himself tried and tested by the Jewish nation's responses to their wilderness experience. He is not pleased with their choices. Let us also consider that He observes us in our wilderness walk as well. He is less than satisfied if our actions resemble those spoken of here in **Hebrews 3**. Showing His displeasure in **Hebrews 3:10(NIV)**, He says, "*I was angry with that generation.*" Emotionally invested and disappointed, we can understand why He continues saying, "*Their hearts are always going astray.*" **Hebrews 3:13(NKJV)**, "*but exhort one another daily, while it is called TODAY, lest any of you be hardened through the deceitfulness.*" It happens in the wilderness. **Hebrews 3:16-19(NIV)**, "*Who were they who heard and rebelled? Were they not all those Moses led out of Egypt? And with whom was He angry for forty years? Was it not with those who sinned, whose bodies perished in the wilderness? And to whom did God swear that they would never enter His rest if not to those who disobeyed? They were not able to enter because of their unbelief.*" There it is folks! That is how Satan tried to disarm Jesus, as well. That is precisely how He will try to disable you. Verse nineteen illuminates Satan's agenda for you. Understand his ultimate objective in your wilderness walk is to bring you to the point of unbelief. Do not let him! Satan has a purpose! He has a goal! He has an agenda!

Know that it is not a coincidence that you find yourself there.

It is not by chance you are having difficulties to the extent of extreme discomfort, or worse. Beware! Satan's goal is to separate you from the living God in your wilderness walk. Also understand, however, you have an opportunity of conquest. Like Jesus, you can destroy the works of the devil too! Know that Satan will try to negate that. He will try to use hardened hearts, rebellion, and so much more to get us to test and try the Holy Spirit, that He would be angry with us as with that generation. Satan wants our hearts to go astray, where we would not know God's ways, where He would declare an oath, and never enter His rest, where sin's deceitfulness hardens us. But understand this! Satan has no authority over you unless you yield it to him. It is all by my choice in the wilderness, and I choose Jesus!

Let us take note all this happened to the Jewish people in their wilderness walk. Let us take note that the lesson for us is that without our understanding of the shared truths above, we can fall into the same satanic ruse as they. It is in our wilderness walk where we are vulnerable as well. If we find ourselves in the same scenario, we too may fall into the trap of Satan's sin. They lost their identity as children of God. The result of identity lost to Satan was the Holy Spirit's anger. The result of anger was that He restricted them from His rest. That rest was in the Promised Land, which is called Canaan, which is now called Israel. Do not allow that to happen to you! **Numbers 14:30(NKJV)**, *"Except for Caleb the son of Jephunneh and Joshua the son of Nun, you shall by no means enter the land which I swore I would make you dwell in."* **Numbers 26:65(NKJV)**, *" for the Lord had said of them, 'They shall surely die in the wilderness. So there was not left a man of them, except Caleb, son of Jephunneh and Joshua son of Nun."* Not even Moses entered. **Joshua 5:6(AMPC)**, *"For the Israelites walked* **(How long)** *forty years* **(Where)** *in the wilderness till* **(What happened)** *all who were men of war who came out of Egypt perished.* **(Why)** *because they did not hearken* *to the voice of the Lord.*" Tested are our hearts in the wilderness. It is where we can rebel, where we can try the Holy Spirit, where He can become angry with us, where we can go astray, and where we may never enter His rest.

As I look back, these questions I posed to myself in my wilderness experiences could have led to temptations. Why do I not see any resolution to my problems? Why am I having constant difficulties unfold over a long period? Why are the issues I am having so intense?" We can find the answers to these questions in more questions. How much or how well have I submitted, and to what extent am I in obedience? **Isaiah 1:19(NKJV)** *"If you are willing and obedient, you shall eat the good of the land."* All but two individuals of that whole generation of Jewish people that came out of Egypt died in the wilderness. If they had been submissive and obedient, they would have entered the promised land and eaten the good of the land of milk and honey. It was the Jewish people's disobedience that prevented the Holy Spirit from allowing them to do so.

CHAPTER 16

They Did Not Enter. They Could Not Enter.

Exodus 23:22(NKJV), *"But if you indeed obey His voice and do all that I speak, then I will be an enemy to your enemies and an adversary to your adversaries."* Let us also understand their children; the second generation, going in, did not have the promised land given to them without shed blood. They had to fight for it. Selah! They had to conquer the cities of the inhabitants who were already there. Those inhabitants would not give up their lives, their families, their cities, and their belongings without a fight. If the disobedient generation of Jews entered the promised land, they would not have succeeded in these battles because their enemies would not have been the Lord's enemies due to their disobedience. They would not have been able to conquer. They would have failed because the Lord would not have been in covenant with them in their battles.

In **Hebrews 3**, we have seen the Holy Spirit emotionally invested. The first generation disobeyed. They received their wages of sin, which is death in the wilderness. Let us understand; however, the Holy Spirit was upset because the Jewish nation would not be prepared to conquer going into the promised land. They would not be able to win in battle. In their wilderness walk, He was attempting to prepare them to come out of the wilderness in His power, the power of the Holy Spirit so they could conquer the land the Father promised them.

It is interesting to note that the Holy Spirit did not give them a vengeful death in the wilderness, in their disobedience. His anger stated in Hebrews 3 was because of frustration and disappointment. He just let them live out their life and pass on. Scattered were their bodies throughout the wilderness. However, let us understand that if He allowed them to go ahead in disobedience, the Lord's will for the land we now call Israel, from that point on until eternity, would have been lost because they would have failed to conquer in their battles. Not only did the disobedient first generation not enter, but they also could not enter. History would have changed. The eternal glory mentioned in **II Corinthians 4:17(NKJV)**, would not have been possible. It states, *"For our light affliction, which is but for a moment, is working for us a far more exceeding and eternal weight of glory."* Among many other events, the life of Jesus and all He had accomplished would have changed because that first generation could not have entered the promised land. All the glory in the land of Israel from that point to today and beyond would have changed. It is because of their disobedience. The Holy Spirit would not have allowed them in.

Disobedience in the wilderness, or anywhere else, can be a precursor of sin. Sin is the reason Satan challenged Jesus' identity for forty days in His wilderness walk. Satan's agenda was for sin to result from trials and temptations. He hoped sin would be the eventuality if Jesus did not place His identity in the Father. Satan knew if Jesus sinned, He surely could not fulfill what the Lord created Him to be. The good news, however, is that we can see Satan's agenda is exposed, and we, now being informed, can respond! The Lord is unfolding this understanding so we can recognize and ultimately be the aggressor that we may come out of our wilderness walk too. With obedience intact, we can see our ability to come out is simply by our choice. To bring obedience into our life enables our enemies to become the Lord's enemies, thus enabled to conquer our promised land, which is our victory walk beyond our wilderness. Yes, we see the Holy Spirit emotionally invested in the Jewish nation's decisions, and being so, He fervently responds to their sin. Did the Holy Spirit want the Jewish people to come out? The answer, of course, is yes, but what is His reason? He wanted them to go into the promised land. Did the Holy Spirit want Jesus to come out of the wilderness? Again, the answer is yes, but why? In **Isaiah 61**, Isaiah prophesied that He wanted Him to come out to go into ministry to fulfill His destiny. Does the Holy Spirit want you to come out of the wilderness? The answer is a resounding yes. But also understand that He and the Father have an agenda for you in the wilderness as well. He wants to put an end to your suffering, despair, fear, and every problematic experience you incur in the wilderness. The Lord also wants you to walk through and come out to fulfill who He has created you to be, in your promised land. He wants you to go in for a while, learn a few things, and come out in power. Understand, this is the process; this is His plan; this is His heart toward you and me. It is His agenda for you in your wilderness.

Can you personalize this to your own life? The failure to obey is why many of us linger in our wilderness walk. Therefore, the length of your stay might depend on your choices there. The nation of Israel rebelled in the wilderness for forty years. They walked around four times in circles in that geographical desert and never came out. They did not submit. They did not obey. In our submission, however, if we obey, our enemies become His enemies, and our adversaries become His adversaries. The Lord's will was realized for the second generation of Israel. The Lord's will is achieved in their obedience. Eternal glory was available in their obedience. Now because of your obedience, the Lord's will for you and me will have eternal significance in the kingdom of God as well! Victory is dependent upon your obedience. Do you know you are an eternal being in Christ? Who knows the achievements He has in store for us here on earth and beyond? It is all dependent on our obedience and the events that are in play because of it!

If you find yourself in a life of disobedience now, considering our Lord's amazing grace, there is still an opportunity to initiate eternal glory today. If you are walking in disobedience now and wish to place submission in your heart, know you can launch eternal glory in your life today. Understand there is an opportunity for your enemies to be the Lord's enemies. He is waiting with open arms. If you wish that eternal glory in your life, then please repeat this prayer:

Our Lord Jesus, thank you for your precious Word and your unfailing love that brings it to me today. I realize now that in my wilderness walk, I have disobeyed. Because of my disobedience, I have sinned. I am sorry for those decisions and repent of those actions. Please forgive me? I understand now that my enemies are your enemies, and my adversaries are your adversaries if I obey. Holy Spirit, please help me see when obedience is a choice, and then I will choose to submit to you. Then I will expect my enemies to bend their knee to you as I come out of my wilderness. Come into my life now. Empower me as I go forward from this day for the rest of my life. I submit to you in Jesus' name. Amen!

CHAPTER 17

You Now Have a Choice

The Door of Full Surrender
TGIF Today God Is First Volume 1 by Os Hillman, Saturday,
August 02, 2014

"But He knows the way that I take; when He has tested me, I will come forth as gold" **Job 23:10(NIV)**. Mr. Hillman poses an interesting scenario. What if we had a choice between choosing God's complete will for our lives as we would want it or submitting to God's whole will? What would be your choice? He says we want to be obedient to the Lord, but are we willing to do it to the extent of surrendering everything to Him. Are you ready to yield everything to Him, without restrictions, yielding all to do whatever He wants? Mr. Hillman states, "If we desire to walk with Christ fully, there is a cost. We may give intellectual assent and go along with His principles and do fine; however, if we entirely are given over to Him and His will for our life, it will be a life that will have adversity." This scenario parallels one reason we have problems mentioned earlier in this text. We can see examples throughout scripture that sin must be broken in our lives to achieve greatness. He says this requires a nature change in us,

not just a change of habits. A nature change can be an excruciating process. Mr. Hillman's thoughts are if God has plans of greatness in your life, your trials may be greater than most. He tells us that, "Your calling may have such responsibility that God cannot afford to entrust it to you without ensuring your complete faithfulness to the calling." His point is that we should not be afraid of this walk, but "embrace it." He suggests this walk may be necessary to fulfill that special place in life God has for you.

He is talking about the Lord trusting us. Our Lord wants to know if He can trust us beyond the wilderness, and He determines that while we are in the wilderness! **II Cor. 4:17(NIV),** "*For our light and momentary troubles are achieving for us an eternal glory that far outweighs them all.*" It is not pretty. It is not pleasant. Yes, it is the door to full surrender. Do not fear the path. Embrace it! Where do we do that? We do that in the wilderness and beyond.

Let us understand the only choice in our trials is to either place our identity as the Lord's in our wilderness or ultimately succumb to Satan's treachery. **I Corinthians 10:5(NKJV).** "*But with most of them God was not well pleased, for their bodies were scattered in the wilderness.*" For you and me, the result of a wrong choice in our wilderness walk is death as well, whether natural, spiritual, relational, or otherwise. Wilderness choices are no small decisions. Know, however, our Lord is now revealing this message for you and me to understand our options. He is giving us knowledge, so we can understand that we have choices. Now, in *Road Map Through the Wilderness*, He answers the following questions that we all have while there. Am I not good enough? Did I do something wrong? Is there anything I can do to get beyond my wilderness experience? What is wrong with me? Know that He is shedding light so you can walk out. Know church, that your plight in your wilderness has not gone unnoticed. You now have a choice!

CHAPTER 18

You Are an Intimidator

In making that choice, it is beneficial to understand the tactics of the enemy as he presents himself. Understanding gives us an advantage. **Luke 4:5-7(AMPC)**, *Then the devil took Him up to a high mountain and showed Him all the kingdoms of the (habitable) world (earth) in a moment of time [[c]in the twinkling of an eye]. And he said to Him, "To You I will give all this power and authority and their glory, (all their magnificence, excellence, preeminence, dignity, and grace), for it has been turned over to me, and I give it to whomever I will. Therefore if You will do homage to and worship me, [[d]just once], it shall all be Yours."* As we look closer at Satan's second temptation, we see a rather generous offer to Jesus. He is offering Jesus all power and authority and glory over everything he has. There has got to be a catch. His obvious objective here is to get Jesus to *"do homage and worship,"* him. That is to worship Satan instead of the Father. Doing so would negate who Jesus was in the Father, thus, changing Jesus' identity from the Son of God to the son of Satan. Here Satan offers authority as well as identity by requesting worship. We can learn some amazing truths as we understand these words Satan uses, with identity being the very target Satan is challenging. By looking closely at Satan's offer, let us examine how these words interact with each other.

Definitions.net defines WORSHIP as "obsequious or submissive respect, extravagant adoration, to honor with extravagant love and extreme submission, as a lover, to adore, to idolize." Worship is not a new concept to us as we already participate in worshiping our Lord. We honor Him as God. We love and adore Him. We give Him respect by submitting ourselves to Him. We are devoted to Him. Every morning my wife and I read our devotional and, by doing so, have devotions. We idolize Him. We worship Him. Satan, however, is enticing Jesus to worship him instead of the Father.

Dictionary.com defines IDENTITY as "the state or fact of being the same as one described." There is a young boy I know who has become quite fond of Batman. He wears Batman socks, Batman pajamas, Batman tee shirts, and anything related to Batman. In his playtime, he imitates Batman in his body movements, and even sounds come out of his mouth, resembling what he perceives as Batman sounds. Although he is not old enough and mature enough to worship Batman, we can undoubtedly see demonstrations of placing his identity as Batman. As he watches Batman demonstrated on various methods of media, he is attempting to be the "same as one described," identity. And a credit to his parents who are doing an excellent job in directing that enthusiasm toward Jesus.

Satan's mindset is to get Jesus to place His identity in him. In doing so, this will replace God as Father and put Satan as Jesus' god. Satan is enticing Jesus to choose himself as Jesus' god. In doing so, Jesus will take on a new identity. If we look closely, we can see Satan is describing lordship. Understanding this, the catalyst for identity (lordship), is through worship. In this one act of worship, Jesus would have been negated as the Son of the Father because He would have lost identity as Son.

Dictionary.com defines AUTHORITY as, *"The right to control, command, or determine."* In **Luke 4** above, Satan says, *"To You I will give all this power and authority and their glory, (all their magnificence, excellence, preeminence, dignity, and grace), for it has been turned over to me, and I give it to whomever I will."* Satan is offering Jesus everything he has. In theory, he is not only saying worship me. The implication is for Jesus to bow a knee to him in subjection. Doing so places His identity with Satan. He is saying that if Jesus comes to him to bow down, having authority over all his kingdoms, having control over them, Satan will give all that he has to Jesus. He says, *"I will give it to you!"* Satan offers to provide Jesus with the power and authority to control and command to give him his authority over everything he has. He says, *"worship me, [[d]just once], it shall all be Yours."*

We can see this same concept illustrated in the natural. If a high school student desires to become a police officer, he or she does not just graduate from high school and instantly become a police officer. There is a process. The graduate must apply to the police department desired, whether it be federal, state, or city. Once accepted, they do not become a police officer immediately. They must submit to rigorous physical training. One must learn techniques about how to protect themselves on the job from perpetrators. A study must be applied to understand the law as it applies to a police officer's duties. Still, they have yet to become police officers. They must take tests with passing scores recorded to authenticate qualification. They walk across the graduation stage, accepting their diploma, and still, they are not police officers. It is not until they take their oath, submit themselves, and take possession of their badge awarded them, receiving authority of the government they represent. Then they become an officer. It is not until they officially receive the authority that they become authorized. They choose to become a police officer years before they qualify. Still, identity and authority do not come to full fruition until they complete training and testing until they receive authority from the governing body. Authority needs to be given and received. The one to whom we place identity is the one from whom we receive authority, in the natural and spiritual.

> WORSHIP - "obsequious or submissive respect, extravagant adoration: to honor with extravagant love and extreme submission, as a lover, to adore, to idolize.: "Satan says, *"If you worship me."*

> IDENTITY- "the state or fact of being the same as one being described." Satan is describing lordship, which is himself as Jesus' god, as His father.

> AUTHORITY- "The right to control, command, or determine:" He will give it to Jesus.

If you (Honor me as god, give submissive respect, idolize), WORSHIP me, Satan says, you will (be the same as described.) Satan is describing himself becoming Jesus' god, lordship, IDENTITY. And if you place your identity in me, you will receive (control and right to command everything I have), my AUTHORITY.

If you WORSHIP me, you will place your IDENTITY in me, and if you place your IDENTITY in me, you will receive my AUTHORITY. We now see Satan's real motive. If you have my AUTHORITY, you cannot have the Father's AUTHORITY. And if you do not have the Father's AUTHORITY, you cannot fulfill **I John 3:8b(NKJV)**, which says, *"The Son of God appeared for this purpose, to destroy the works of the devil."* And here we see it again. Satan wants to render Jesus ineffective. He intends to diffuse Him because Jesus is a significant threat to Satan.

By Jesus' example, we can now understand the opportunity

available to us in the Kingdom of God. If we can see these truths in the interaction between Satan and Jesus, we can understand these same truths already established between Jesus and the Father. Truth, as it applies to God's kingdom, is also a truth for Satan's kingdom. Understanding that the one to whom we place our identity is the one from whom we receive authority, by putting our identity in the Father, we receive the AUTHORITY of the Father. Selah!

Understanding Jesus is now with you, understanding that you have placed your identity as Jesus' brother or sister, Satan will attempt to negate your identity. Satan will try to deceive you and tempt you from continuing your walk in the authority you already have as Christ's. Satan will offer you the things of this world. Which would you prefer? Is it fame, riches, power, glory, authority? He will give you whatever you want in his kingdom. What is the catch? You are required to place your identity in him and give up your identity in the Father, Son, and Holy Ghost, IN THE WILDERNESS! He wants to steal away your identity as son/daughter of the Father, the identity He gave you when you chose Christ. And like his attempt at Jesus' identity, Satan wants to render you ineffective to the cause of Jesus. He plans to change our identity that we also cannot destroy his works.

Here is the good news. We are now informed! We can know and understand **WHAT** Satan is trying to do. That is to change our identity. **HOW** he does it is by unbelief. **WHERE** he will try to do it is in your wilderness. **I Peter 5:8(NKJV)**, *"Be sober, be vigilant; because your adversary the devil walks about like a roaring lion, seeking whom he may devour."* **WHY** is that? It is because Satan is afraid of Jesus! Satan is afraid of you! Satan is intimidated by Jesus! Satan is intimidated by you in Jesus. It is because you, also, are called to *"destroy the works of the devil"* **I John 3:8b(NKJV)**. That is because you are *"predestined to conform to the image of Christ"* **Romans 8:29(NKJV)**. Can you grab the magnitude of that truth? Can you just get a small glimpse of how the Father sees you from His eyes, understanding the identity He has of you, an intimidator to the kingdom of darkness? No other time or place in Jesus' life did Satan go on the offensive except the wilderness and the cross. No other place in your life will he go on the attack, except the wilderness, understanding that you will not need to endure the cross, payment of sin, because Jesus has already done so for you. The wilderness is Satan's only opportunity to break your identity in our Lord, and now he is exposed!

I find it a little comical that Satan, offering this temptation to Jesus, has recorded in the Bible the very truth that is ultimately the root of his demise. That is, WORSHIP places IDENTITY, and to IDENTIFY with our Lord brings His AUTHORITY. We, His church, can now understand that truth and apply it with the same results as Jesus. As we grasp this concept, let us focus on the significance of what the Lord is offering us, the church. I heard someone describe the majesty of our Lord, saying that He was so grand He needs to bend over to see the universe. That is a universe of billions of solar systems. If we place our identity in the Father, we receive the AUTHORITY of none other than the Father. Selah! You have the authority of the one who parted the Red Sea, the authority of the one who took a rib from Adam and created Eve, the one who sits on the throne of heaven itself and reigns over all creation. You have the authority of the Father!

CHAPTER 19

Knowing Your Enemy Breaks Up the Depths

Luke 4:13(NKJV), *"Now when the devil had ended every temptation, he departed from Him until an opportune time."* He tried every trick in the book. He has already lost, but he has not figured that out yet! It is up to you and me to show him. It starts as a process in the wilderness. Choosing brings worship; worship brings identity; identity brings submission; submission brings authority; authority brings power. Here is the beauty of what the Lord is revealing to us. We do not have to be idle in the wilderness. We can do something about Satan's wilderness attacks! **Proverbs 3: 19-20(NKJV)**, *"The Lord by wisdom founded the earth; By understanding, He established the heavens; By His knowledge, the depths were broken up."* And with this knowledge, the Lord is revealing to us that Satan is now exposed. His tactics are now known.

In the movie, The Patriot, Mel Gibson played the part of Benjamin Martin. It takes place in the south during the Revolutionary War. Benjamin Martin is a Colonel in the colonial militia, fighting the Red Coats. In a raid on a country road, his band of militia captured General Cornwallis's notes of previous battles. By studying those, Benjamin Martin was able to learn how Cornwallis thought, of his tactics, and particularly his weakness'. In this case, it was pride. Thus, he was able to devise a battleplan, which resulted in a defeat that ultimately turned the direction of the war to Cornwallis' full surrender. He did this by obtaining knowledge of his enemy, and he used that to his advantage and Cornwallis' disadvantage, unto Cornwallis' defeat!

Now that the Lord is illuminating this wilderness topic, we can understand Satan's weakness' in the wilderness. In like manner to the scenario above with Benjamin Martin and Cornwallis, we can use this knowledge the Lord is sharing with us to Satan's disadvantage unto defeat, and the advantage of the kingdom and ourselves. THANK YOU, LORD, FOR KNOWLEDGE!

Why is it good to know about breaking up the depths? Why is it essential that we spend all this time talking about Satan? John Hagee wrote a book called *"The Three Heavens."* He quotes an ancient Chinese military genius named Sun Tzu. According to Wikipedia, "Sun Tzu was a Chinese general, writer, military strategist, and philosopher. He wrote the book, *The Art of War*, a work of military strategy that affected Western and Eastern Asian philosophy and military thinking. It is accepted as a masterpiece on strategy and has been frequently cited and referred to by generals and strategists. Sun Tzu is revered in Chinese and East Asian culture as a legendary historical and military figure." In his book, *The Three Heavens*, John Hagee quotes Sun Tzu saying, "If you know the enemy and yourself, you need not fear the result of 100 battles. If you know yourself but not the enemy, for every victory, you will also suffer a defeat. If you know neither the enemy nor yourself, you will succumb in every battle." Know your enemy, church. Retain this knowledge that *"breaks up the depths!"* In the same book, John Hagee also speaks of Gen. George Patton, "Patton, however, realized the truth that many Christians choose to dis-regard: to know your enemy is to process the power to defeat him." In the old west, the Indians sent out scouts. America invented radar in World War II. Now we have satellites positioned in space, orbiting our globe. All of these are to gather information so we can know our enemy.

It is by understanding these truths that we now make this profound conclusion. We now have knowledge of our enemy, and we can use that to his disadvantage because *"The hypocrite with his mouth destroys his neighbor. but through knowledge the righteous will be delivered"* **Proverbs 11:9(NKJV)**.

In using this knowledge, Jesus, coming out of the wilderness in the power of the Holy Spirit, has graduated! He is qualified! He has earned His kingdom PhD. in the ministry of the Messiah! He brought out of the wilderness the one thing that qualified Him for ministry. That is the Father's authority. The amazing fact is that coming out, we have that same authority available as well. With this authority, however, we are not called to command and control flesh and blood. The church is not called to be warriors in the flesh but to be lambs and servants. However, we have the right to command and control the ones who try to influence flesh and blood negatively. Those are principalities, powers, and rulers of darkness. **Colossians 2:15(NKJV)**, tells us, *"Having disarmed principalities and powers, He made a public spectacle of them, triumphing over them in it,"* (the cross). **Ephesians 4:14(NKJV)**, *"that we should no longer be children, tossed to and fro and carried about with every wind of doctrine."* The Lord is now giving us knowledge and understanding. **Proverbs 3:20(NKJV)**, *"By His knowledge the depths were broken up."* **Hosea 4:6(NKJV)**, *"My people are destroyed for lack of knowledge."* The simple truth is this. We will either break up the depths using the knowledge He has given us, or be destroyed, for the lack of using it. It is all based on choice. It is the church knowing who our opposition is, Satan. And yes, there is going to be a fight!

CHAPTER 20

Are You A General Yet?

Dr. Mike Murdock authoring *Wisdom Talk -Morning Motivation* says, "War is the seed of possessions. The spoils of war are worth the battle. When David defeated Goliath, he was fully aware of the rewards King Saul would bestow upon the champion. Men fight for a reason – to gain something they want. In the Kingdom of God, battle decides rank." **Hebrews 12:2(NKJV)**, "*Who for the joy that was set before Him endured the cross.*" Jesus has rank. Billy Graham has rank in the kingdom of God. Many pastors have rank. And now, the opportunity for rank is placed before you. Are you ready for a promotion?

Psalms 37:39-40(NKJV), "*But the salvation of the righteous is from the Lord; He is their strength in the time of trouble. And the Lord shall help them and deliver them; He shall deliver them from the wicked and save them because they trust in him.*" Salvation in battle is based on trust when we are fighting the darkness! Yes, I must have faith, but when I am fighting darkness, knowledge also helps me trust.

Having obtained trust, I can see that I have an opportunity in the wilderness, not despair, not wondering what is wrong with me, not wondering if I did something wrong, not guessing if God has rejected me, and not guessing if there is a God. **Deuteronomy 8:13(NKJV)**"*And the Lord will make you the head and not the tail; you shall be above only and not be beneath, if you heed the commandments of the Lord.*" When you find yourself in the wilderness, you have the opportunity to be observant, the opportunity to understand. Therefore, you can see your enemy and the chance to have the Lord fight for you. I remember from years ago when I discovered this truth. I found myself speaking out in prayer, "Satan, I see you in the wilderness!" **Deuteronomy 20:1-4(NKJV)** *"When you go out to battle against your enemies, and see horses and chariots and people more numerous than you, therefore do not be afraid of them; for the Lord your God is with you, who brought you up from the land of Egypt. So it shall be, when you are on the verge of battle, that the priest shall approach and speak to the people. And he shall say to them, 'Hear, O Israel: Today you are on the verge of battle with your enemies. Do not let your heart faint, do not be afraid, and do not tremble or be terrified because of them; for the Lord your God is He who goes with you, to fight for you against your enemies, to save you."* Now, with Jesus illuminating the wilderness, seeing your enemy, the good news is He gives you the opportunity. He will go with you, and he will fight for you. That does not mean you will not be involved. That does not mean you will not get a spiritual "bloody nose." It does mean the Lord will reveal what to do about that opportunity because He will give you rank.

Nothing happens, however, without the Father's authority. The Father starts this process by sharing this TRUTH established earlier. The one in whom we place our identity is the one from whom we receive authority. But Jesus did not worship Satan. He did not put His identity in Satan. Jesus did not receive authority from Satan. That means since Jesus placed His identity as Son in the Father, He received the Father's authority. He said no thank you to Satan's offer, but He accepted the identity as the Son of the Father. How? By his own choice.

Jesus was filled with the Holy Spirit by the river but had no authority there. He received the Father's authority in the wilderness. For this reason, Jesus did not immediately go into ministry when the Holy Spirit fell on Him. On the riverbank, after baptism, the Holy Spirit gave Him his tools for His toolbox, but Jesus was still not yet prepared. Jesus did not have all the qualities that he needed to fulfill all that Isaiah prophesied about Him in **Isaiah 61**. He was still not fully equipped to walk in the ministry prophesied for Him.

Isaiah 61:1-3(NKJV), *"the Spirit of the Lord God is upon me, because the Lord has anointed me to preach good tidings to the poor; he has sent me to heal the brokenhearted, to proclaim liberty to the captives, and the opening of the prison to those who are bound; to proclaim the acceptable year of the Lord, and the day of vengeance of our God; to comfort all who mourn in Zion, to give them beauty for ashes, the oil of Joy for morning, the garment of praise for the spirit of heaviness."* With the fullness of the Holy Spirit and the authority of the Father, Jesus can now go forth and deal with Satan. He is now qualified in the wilderness and beyond. Understand the invitation is for you to be qualified as well. Also, having the fullness of the Holy Spirit and authority of the Father, you are called to come out of the wilderness, go forth and face Satan going on into your called ministry. That ministry happens in the wilderness and beyond. Jesus needed the opportunity to choose His own identity as Son, even though He heard the Father speak it just after being baptized. In the wilderness He needed the opportunity to place His own identity in the Father to receive that authority. The catalyst of power is the Father's authority, and Jesus had to go into the wilderness to get it. Being legitimately predestined to be conformed to the image of Christ, this same process applies to you and me to come out of our wilderness experience in power. Having the Father's authority enables you to do that. Yes, you, too, can be qualified, having received the Father's authority!

Luke 4:14(AMPC), *"Then Jesus went back full of and under the power of the [Holy] Spirit into Galilee, and the fame of Him spread through the whole region round about."* Jesus' ministry was not evident until after He came out of the wilderness. He had no fame until He came out of the wilderness. His fame was because he had power. He had power because He walked out of the wilderness with the Father's authority! To fulfill what the Father created Him to be, He had to come through the wilderness! As do you!

We can now see the Trinity working in tandem. The Father gives Jesus identity at baptism. Jesus chooses the identity of the Father and submits. The Father then gives Jesus His authority, enabling the Holy Spirit's power to go forth by speaking the Word. When Jesus spoke the Word, kingdom events occurred. Spiritual sparks flew. You can speak the Word unto power as well and make things happen in our Lord with His authority.

CHAPTER 21

Authority Allows Me to Thrive.

Some have asked why I have a whitetail deer on Road Map's shield. The reason is that I spend much time in the woods and fields hunting deer. Unfortunately, I do much more hunting than I do getting. In those quiet times in His creation, the Lord has revealed His truths to me numerous times. The following experience illustrates His heart for you and me.

A local farmer approached me about hunting on his property. He said the deer population was high, and they were causing significant crop damage. I spoke with my hunting buddy, and we quickly responded, saying yes before the farmer changed his mind. Several days later, while walking around his fields, we came to a small field with an abundant, lush crop of soybeans. The plants were so healthy that the top leaves were well above my belt line. It was disheartening when I saw three separate trails coming from three different directions out of the woods into the field. Each path led well into the center, where the deer helped themselves to the beautiful stand of soybeans. At the end of each trail, a large circle of plant stubs was only several inches high. Each damaged area was approximately one quarter acre in size, with each having the leaves and stalks eaten near the ground. My estimate of the damage in that field was about thirty-five percent, which would erode his harvest by about thirty-five percent, which would have taken most of his profit. Considering these signs, my friend Art and I were quickly watching that field. The first evening, Art saw only one deer at dusk, and I saw none. Over several watches following, no deer had arrived. Both of us were getting confused and discouraged. That evening Art decided to watch another area. I realized we had not prayed before our previous hunting outings and suggested we do so. My prayer was not long or elaborate. I just asked the Lord if we could enjoy His creation that evening. Art went on to his location, and I found a small area behind a tree that would be good cover for me to blend into the background. About forty-five minutes before sunset, my peripheral vision picked up a quick movement, which revealed several deer dashing into a tree line from a standing crop of corn.

All I saw were three forms with no significant detail running about Seventy yards away from me. Only after five minutes elapsed a magnificent ten-point buck came out of the woods into the soybean field. His antlers were massive, high, and wide with both of his brow tines, the small antlers directly above his head, displaying a Y. They are quite unusual. He was slowly walking toward me with antlers sparkling in the evening sun, and occasionally leaning down to take a bite of soybean leaves. Approximately ten minutes later, from the same area, another beautiful buck walked into the field. Although he was not quite the trophy, he was a beautiful deer in his own right, carrying eight points above his head. Pulling up the scope, I noticed the second deer moving slightly faster through the field toward the first, eventually coming near enough that I was able to see both in my scope at the same time.

Approximately Fifteen minutes elapsed, still watching these two most beautiful animals, a third one slowly walked into my vision from a near position at my left. I was seeing all three standing in front of me, and I saw all three through the scope at the same time. Amazingly, this third deer was massive. Antlers were not as high as the other two but extremely wide, unusually wide from others I have seen. Later, the farmer told me he nicknamed him Bullwinkle, named after the cartoon character, Bullwinkle the Moose. The fantastic thing about this incident is that I would have felt blessed to see any of these deer in their natural habitat during one lifetime. I would consider myself blessed if I had the opportunity to see these three animals over ten lifetimes. But here stood all three, all in line in my scope, at the very same time. Chuckling as I walked back to my truck while feeling most grateful, it occurred to me that not only did I pray earlier, but I prayed that I could enjoy His creation. The Lord's response to my prayer enabled me to thrive in my experience that evening. Of course, the Lord has a sense of humor. As I admired these beautiful deer feeding in the evening sunlight, I was limited to only watching them for those forty-five minutes as it was the first day of the doe season.

I did not see the real significance of the evening events until Sunday morning in praise time at church when the praise team sang these words from the song *Thrive* by Casting Crowns. "We were not made just to survive, but we were made to thrive." I had witnessed the evening before, the highlight of this outdoorsman's life in God's creation. I was able to see that our Lord desires to be active in our lives. Even so in the smallest of things. He also demonstrated that He wishes me to thrive far more than I could ever imagine; He only awaits my invitation.

I would be the first to tell you that I did not thrive in my wilderness situations. It is most challenging to thrive in the Lord when in the wilderness, under Satan's influence. Get out! Get away from that influence. Obtain the authority of the Father so you can thrive in who He has created to be. **Mark 1:28(NKJV)**, *"and immediately His fame spread throughout all the region around*

Galilee." Coming out of the wilderness, He immediately became famous. Jesus was not really known, except for impressing a few people in the synagogue when He was twelve years old. It was not His time yet.

When He exited the wilderness, however, with power, anointed, and sent, having received the Father's authority, He became famous. It was the wilderness experience that catapulted Him into His ministry. That's why we go through the wilderness also. We, too, can obtain authority so that we can thrive, so we, too, can walk in the power of the Holy Spirit, anointed, and sent. The Lord has created us for this walk. It is our destiny to be just like Jesus. The Father wants us to thrive! All is made possible for us when carrying His authority. Choosing Jesus brings the process of worship. Worshiping Him enables identity in Him. Placing identity in Him brings submission. Submitting to Him brings the authority of the Father. Authority is the catalyst for power in the kingdom of God. It all becomes a reality in the wilderness to fulfill who He created you to be, in Jesus. Know that He has predestined you to thrive!

CHAPTER 22

Run to the Battle Line

Trained for War
TGIF *Today God Is First* Volume 2 by Os Hillman Tuesday, May 19, 2015

"Praise be to the Lord my Rock, who trains my hands for war, my fingers for battle" **Psalm 144:1(NIV)**. Mr. Hillman states that having Bible knowledge only, we will never experience God in powerful ways. "It is only when we use that knowledge in the heat of battle that you will know the reality of what you've learned intellectually." "Otherwise," He says, "it yields little fruit and remains only an exercise in spiritual gymnastics." He explains that David, as a shepherd fighting wild animals, was a training ground for his battle with Goliath.

He indicates that many local churches, "are designed to tickle the ears," that many look like luxury cruise liners entertaining their members to make them feel good. Agreeing with him, he states that it is time that our churches now should look like battleships designed to train an army for war. The preparation for this war does not resemble a war in the natural but one of a spiritual nature. We agree that too many of us are watching from the sideline, especially in the scenario, the world's ruler, Satan, places us in today.

He points out that in sports, it is not until we enter the competition, that we discover how well we handle the pressure. You can practice all you want, but you never know how to do it until you enter the game, testing what you have learned. He says, "In battle, you discover how well you are trained by what you do on the battlefield."

David learned well in his training as the shepherd fighting bears and lions in the field. The true test was when he faced the giant Goliath on the battlefield. It is generally accepted that the interaction between David and Goliath illustrates the interaction between darkness and light. What better example do we have of darkness and light interaction than Jesus and Satan in the wilderness. By looking closely at the David/Goliath story, we can understand more about the interaction between Jesus and Satan. In doing so, we can discover some truths that apply to us as we face the darkness in our wilderness experience.

It is more than a coincidence that Goliath's boasting, challenging, and tempting lasted forty days, the same number of days Jesus interacted with Satan. **I Samuel 17:16(NKJV),** *"And the Philistine drew near and presented himself forty days, morning and evening.*

I Samuel 17:41-47(NIV), *"Meanwhile, the Philistine, with his shield bearer in front of him, kept coming closer to David. He looked David over and saw that he was little more than a boy, glowing with health and handsome, and he despised him. He said to David, "Am I a dog that you come at me with sticks?" And the Philistine cursed David by his gods. "Come here, he said, "and I'll give your flesh to the birds and the wild animals!"* If we read these words carefully, we can determine the heart of Goliath's rantings. We can grasp his arrogance, evil extending from curses, contempt, hatred, and pride. *David said to the*

Philistine, *"You come against me with sword and spear and javelin, but I come against you in the name of the Lord Almighty, the God of the armies of Israel, whom you have defied. This day the Lord will deliver you into my hands, and I'll strike you down and cut off your head. This very day I will give the carcasses of the Philistine army to the birds and the wild animals, and the whole world will know that there is a God in Israel.*

All those gathered here will know that it is not by sword or spear that the Lord saves; for the battle is the Lord's, and he will give all of you into our hands." David responds with boldness, confidence, authority, faith, and the identity of a kingdom warrior. There is your example!

I Samuel 17:48(RSV), *"When the Philistine arose and came and drew near to meet David, David ran quickly toward the battle line to meet the Philistine."* Of the numerous times, I have read this chapter; somehow, I missed these words. David was not a victim. Discussed earlier, Jesus was not a victim. He ran to the battle line. You are not a victim when you choose and run to the battle line! What was David feeling? What emotion was he experiencing? David said, **I Samuel 17:46-47(NKJV)**, *"This day the Lord will deliver you into my hand, and I will strike you and take your head from you. And this day I will give the carcasses of the camp of the Philistines to the birds of the air and the wild beasts of the earth, that all the earth may know that there is a God in Israel."* David did not say, bless your little heart, Goliath. I am going to cut your head off now. He spoke in anger, righteous anger! Look at David's heart. Look at what is going on in his mind. Look at what Spirit he is exhibiting. They are anger, boldness, confidence, identity, and authority.

What brought David to this scene is that his brothers were in the army of Israel. **I Samuel 17:19(NKJV)**, *"Now Saul and they and all the men of Israel were in the Valley of Elah, fighting with the Philistines."* One day David's father wanted to send food to his brothers. After arriving, David's conversation with several soldiers demonstrates the identity he had of himself in the Lord. **I Samuel 17:26b(NKJV)**, *"For who is this uncircumcised Philistine that he should defy the armies of the living God?"* David understands identity. He knows his status. Everyone else is looking at the intimidating giant in fear while David identifies himself as God's own! That is his identity. There's your example, prepared to do battle in the wilderness!

CHAPTER 23

Cut Off His Head

Ephesians 6:10-17(NKJV), *"Finally, my brethren, be strong in the Lord and in the power of His might. Put on the whole armor of God, that you may be able to stand against the wiles (tricks, deception) of the devil. For we do not wrestle against flesh and blood, but against principalities, against powers, against the rulers of the darkness of this age, against spiritual hosts of wickedness in the heavenly places. Therefore take up the whole armor of God, that you may be able to withstand in the evil day, and having done all, to stand. Stand therefore, having girded your waist with truth, having put on the breastplate of righteousness, and having shod your feet with the preparation of the gospel of peace; above all, taking the shield of faith with which you will be able to quench all the fiery darts of the wicked one. And take the helmet of salvation, and the sword of the Spirit, which is the Word of God."* There is much to be said about the full armor of God. For our purpose, we will limit ourselves to one significant concept. Of God's whole armor, there is only one listed that is an offensive weapon. **Ephesians 10:17(NKJV)**, *"the Sword of the Spirit, which is the Word of God."* Of all others, girding our waist, the breastplate, having our feet shod, the shield, and the helmet; none are offensive in nature except the sword. With every temptation that Satan brought to Jesus, His response was always speaking the Word into Satan's treacherous temptations, silencing him, ultimately causing him to leave. *Satan "departed from Him until an opportune time"* **Luke 4:13(NKJV)**. Of significance is that not only did Jesus speak the Word but that Satan had no response. Satan has no power against the Word of God spoken into any scenario where he is present and attempting to control. He had no choice but to leave because the Word negated Satan's ultimate goal, unbelief. The obvious reason is that the Word is truth. Satan only has power over what you give him, except truth. If you only speak out the truth, the Word of God, when He attacks, he has no control. His tools are deception through lies. Therefore, when we speak the truth of God, he has no choice but to leave. He has no counter-play for truth. The truth of the Word negates his lies. The Word of God is the offensive weapon used in any interaction with Satan in a wilderness experience. Using the Sword of the Spirit, the battle is won, implementing His truth.

There is our example! If you see Satan in front of you to challenge your faith, throw the Word in his face. Take that sword and speak it forth, literally, with your audible voice. He cannot stay. He will depart from you for a more opportune time. What Word do I speak forth? There are over five thousand promises in the Bible. **Joshua 1:5(NKJV)**, *"No man shall be able to stand before you all the days of your life; as I was with Moses, so I will be with you. I will not leave you nor forsake you."* **Isaiah 54:17(NKJV)**, *"No weapon formed against you will prosper I will not leave you nor forsake you. And every tongue which rises against you in judgment you shall condemn."* **Deuteronomy 28:13(NKJV)**, *"And the Lord will make you the head and not the tail."* Many more words in scripture can be placed before Satan by your voice. Find them. Memorize them. Be ready for Satan to stick his face in yours. Have the Sword of the Spirit prepared to respond to his fruits, his lies, and his intended deception. Andrew Wommac, TV Bible teacher says, "Don't speak to the Lord about your enemy. Speak to the enemy about your Lord."

Satan wants us to go into the wilderness and stay there, walking in circles like the Jewish nation in their wilderness experience, until our bodies are scattered as well, dead to spiritual life, dead to natural life, dead in unbelief! The Father and the Holy Spirit want us to go into the wilderness for a short time, get His knowledge, receive the Father's authority, and walk out in power, just like Jesus.

Several years ago, I was hunting the same field mentioned in a previous chapter. An old area on the north side was a former field. It was not tilled for several years and neglected. Weeds there were a little less than chest high, along with a few hardwood trees scattered throughout. The trees had little competition for sunlight, so they appeared to resemble large bushes rather than the tall trees one might usually see in a forest. I placed my seat, a five-gallon bucket, next to the soybean field, several feet into the weeds. There I saw a movement about six inches from my left foot. Looking down, I saw the largest black snake I had ever seen. Because blacksnakes are not venomous, I was not alarmed.

Due to the chill in the air, and the snake being a coldblooded animal, it slowly crawled away. Approximately fifteen minutes later, quietly sitting on my chair, and about twenty feet from my position, I saw the snake slowly moving through the branches of the tree beside my head. I suspect it was getting positioned in the tree to take advantage of the warmth from what little sunlight was available at the end of the day. The thought immediately occurred to me, envisioning a machete in my hand, that if that snake wanted to attack me from that position, that is to jump from the tree and land on me, and if it were venomous, I would have no chance to protect myself with the machete. I would be dead. Then in an instant, this thought occurred to me. One cannot cut the head off the serpent when on the defense.

At first, I was startled, wondering, "What exactly does that mean?" Sitting there in the stillness of the evening, I pondered that thought. I remembered learning as a child in my school that a rattlesnake can strike, recoil, and strike three more times before a person has time to react. I also recalled watching in recent months a documentary on television. It was a demonstration of the strike of one the most venomous snakes in the world, the Australian Brown Snake. During the segment, they demonstrated an example of the snake's feeding process; thus, it's striking capability on a field rat. When this snake struck its victim, it was so fast I could barely see it move. The strike was scarcely a blur. And then I understood.

In our wilderness struggles, there is no opportunity to defeat Satan if we take on the identity of a victim. You cannot cut the head off the serpent, Satan, when on the defense. Quite the opposite is true; however, if you take on the identity of an aggressor, you can cut off the head of the serpent on the offense. You can sever the head of the serpent, Satan, on the attack. David demonstrated that by literally cutting off the head of Goliath when he ran to the battle line. Jesus demonstrated being the aggressor by speaking the Word of the Lord, the sword of the Spirit when He responded to Satan's attacks in His wilderness experience. They were both aggressive warriors, not passive victims! But you may say, *Satan is Alive and Well on Planet Earth*, quoting Hal Lindsey's book. That is correct. Satan is not dead. He still is quite active in our lives. Pick up your sword. Run to the battle line! You can cut off the head of the serpent when on the offense in your wilderness experience. You can cut off the serpent's head when you run to the battle line, with the sword of the Spirit, the Word of God!

Mike Murdock Morning Meditation

"Fight for your Harvest ...Through Focused Faith. You have an enemy. Satan wants to steal everything God has for you. Don't let him. Use your weapons,...your words . . .the Word of God. . . your faith . . . To go after the harvest when it is delayed. Satan fears a fighter. Every harvest in your life will require a battle." I have heard it said that Satan wants us to think we are not strong enough to withstand the storm. You are a child of God, a person of faith. You are the storm! Know that truth applies, especially in your wilderness experience.

You are not a victim!
You are a warrior of Christ! Pick up your sword!
Run to the Battle Line! Speak the Word of God!
Cut off the head of the serpent! You are the storm!

CHAPTER 24

Righteous Anger

I have experienced, and others have demonstrated their anger at our Lord while receiving pain that darkness presents. It is easy to blame our God and thus alienate ourselves from Him in misplaced anger. One said to me recently, "If God loves me, He should not let me go through this experience and receive all this pain." Brothers and sisters, He is not the cause of your pain. He is the reliever of your pain!

What then must I do to get out? How long must I stay in the wilderness? We find the answer is in another question. What is it going to take to get you angry? What will it take for you, in leaving back nothing, to place your identity, your whole self, as Christ's? What is it going to take to get you to understand the authority you have available to you? What will it take for you to get you angry enough to stand up to darkness, trying to enslave you and yours? What will it take to stand up to the one trying to kill you and yours? It is righteous anger!

We, the church, have been good students learning how to become lambs and servants in the natural. But how many of us have missed the opportunity to become what David and Jesus became? That is lions with righteous anger in the Spirit? When facing

Goliath, Saul's army was not angry. **I Samuel 17:11(NKJV),** *"When Saul and all Israel heard those words of the Philistine, they were dismayed and greatly afraid."* The word dismay means sudden or complete loss of courage. They were utterly disheartened. This scripture clearly illustrates the emotion they were experiencing was fear. Understand you cannot experience fear and have faith at the same time. They are opposites.

Several years ago, while traveling in the West Virginia mountains, we stopped at a small country store and bought a sign that expressed this very scenario. "Fear stops, where faith begins." The Army of Israel was disabled with fear. David had no fear, having placed his identity in and receiving authority from the Lord. There is our example, church. I quote **I Samuel 17:26b(NKJV)** again regarding his identity in the Lord. *"For who is this uncircumcised Philistine that he should defy the armies of the living God?"*

So, what situation are you experiencing? Is it enough to make you angry? Or is Satan going to place in you, loss of courage, and make you utterly disheartened, ultimately bringing you to the point of unbelief? How many vessels are you going to set out for the Lord to fill? Is the number based on an expectation of multiplication, or is it based on a limitation of expectations? Understand this, church. Satan, by his very nature, will take until you make a stand. In the natural, unless confronted, does a thief stop stealing? No! Does a liar stop lying unless he is caught in his lies and confronted? No! Unless confronted, does a person who destroys marriages, destroys computers with a virus, and destroys the lives of innocent people stop? No! Did Sadam Hussein stop killing, raping, and committing so many other atrocities until he was confronted, tried, and put to death? NO!!!! Evil's appetite will never be satisfied. Your choice is to stand up and fight or be consumed by darkness. It is a confrontation! Our example was when David confronted Goliath and ran to the battle line. Now

Jesus is our example in the wilderness. He did not back down from Satan. He threw the Word of God back to him and sent him away with no effect.

Unless forced to do so, Satan will not bend a knee. Why? It is just his nature. Greed feeds self. Lust of the eyes, the lust of the flesh, and the pride of life are never satisfied. Satan came to steal, kill, and destroy, literally, and his appetites will never stop until he steals all, kills all, and destroys all unless you confront him with the sword of the Spirit, which is the Word of God. And who is in the liar's heart? It is Satan. Who is in the thief 's heart? It is Satan. Who is in a destroyer's heart? It is Satan.

I Samuel 17:46(NKJV), *"I will give the carcasses of the Philistine Army to the birds and wild animals,"* David says. **I Samuel 17:46b(NKJV)**, *"The battle is the Lord's, and he will give all of you into our hands."* That is the heart of a righteous warrior. That is the heart of Jesus in the wilderness battle, and that is the example Jesus gives you and me in our wilderness struggles. What did David use to cut off Goliath's head? It was the sword. What did Jesus use to fight Satan? It was the Word of God, the Bible, which is the sword of the Spirit. In **Matthew 4:4(NKJV)** He says, *"Man does not live by bread alone, but by every Word that proceeds out of the mouth of the God,"* lashing back at Satan. And what is the only part of God's spiritual armor that is an offensive weapon? It is the Sword of the Spirit, which is the Word of God. And what does a sword do? It cuts, slashes, severs, and it kills. And what is the emotion of a natural warrior as a cutter, a slasher, a severer, and a killer? It is anger at his enemy. What is the emotion of a spiritual warrior using the Sword of the Spirit to cut, slash, sever, kill, and destroy the devil's works? It is anger, righteous anger.

Dr. Mike Murdock in *My Wisdom Notes says,*
"Disobedience Is the Seed For Tragedy."

- Dr. Murdock states, *"You must develop a hatred for evil. You Can Only Conquer What You Hate."* He invites us to note all the items in our lives that come against our well-being. He names alcohol, illegal drugs, abortion, and many other actions that destroy thousands of individuals' lives. We all can think of other examples. Acts resulting from deception, abandonment, hate, rage, untruth, and many other actions rooted in sin destroy lives. Dr. Murdock says, "Walk toward God. Walk toward righteousness. You will never regret it." ***Proverbs 8:13(NKJV),*** *"The fear of the Lord is to hate evil."*

CHAPTER 25

It Is Not A Sin

What emotion was Jesus experiencing when he called the Pharisees a brood of vipers? What emotion did Jesus experience when He threw the money changers out of the temple? What was the Holy Spirit experiencing when He said, *"I was angry with that generation,"* in **Hebrews 3:10(NKJV)**, discussed earlier? Anger is the obvious answer. Can Jesus sin? Can the Holy Spirit sin? Of course not. **Ephesians 4:26(NKJV)** says, *"Be angry, and do not sin."* **Joel 2:13(NKJV).** *"For He is gracious and merciful, Slow to anger, and of great kindness; And He relents from doing harm."* Anger is not a sin if it is right standing with God. Anger toward Satan most definitely is righteous anger. If the Lord has demonstrated anger, we as sons and daughters can express anger as well. And we, being sons and daughters displaying anger, need to do so according to the Word of God. We, too, receive righteousness through Jesus. **II Corinthians 5:21(NKJV),** *"For He made Him who knew no sin to be sin for us, that we might become the righteousness of God in Him."*

The *dictionary.com* defines emotionalism as "1. Excessively emotional character 2. Strong or excessive appeal to the emotions 3. A tendency to respond with undue emotions 4. Unwarranted expression or display of emotion." We should not get ourselves worked up with unwarranted or excessive emotion. It is not the act of extreme emotion that brings power to a situation. It is the experience, the feeling within.

Some years ago, my wife and I attended a church where a young man announced his calling as a pastor. After some urging over time, the senior pastor agreed to allow him to bring the message on a Sunday evening. My wife and I were sitting in the second row, listening to a Biblically sound message. As he advanced in his presentation, the young man's delivery progressed. He appeared to be emotional, eventually to be crying. In the sanctuary, in the second row, while sitting relatively near him, I realized that at this heightened point in his message, there were no tears. He was not emotionally involved at all. He was saying the right words but was imitating others he had observed previously, resembling those who were responding with genuine emotion. Indeed, there was no anointing. Indeed, the pastor did not invite him to speak again.

Let us understand an emotional display that is not authentic has no place in the sanctuary, or anywhere else for that matter, if it is not from the Spirit of our Lord if it is not a genuine expression of the heart.

Today, at times, with genuine emotion from feelings within, you and I will be called to be the catalyst for authentic ministry. Many of us display our feelings outwardly. Many of us reveal our emotions more subtly. Our pastor, Rick Betts, repeatedly tells us, "It is all about the heart." It is not how loud we speak. Speaking out, however, may be appropriate. **I John 3:18(NRSV)** says, "*Little children, let us love, not in word or speech, but in truth and action.*" I love in truth and action by giving to those in need. I love with truth and action as I pray for those in turmoil and those in pain; physical, spiritual, and emotional. I love in truth and action by getting angered at Satan and lashing out with the Sword of the Spirit, the Word of God! Yes, we act out at Satan. Yes, we may be emotional. But we serve because of love, not because of some emotional hype. It is ok to get angry at Satan because of the love within us. Satan comes to destroy the very love we have received from the Lord.

"For God so loved the world that he gave..." **John 3:16(NKJV)**, and we are grateful for that love. He gives us a love that provides us with unmerited favor, grace. He provides us with a love that not only pays for our sin, forgives us of our sin, but *"as far as the east is from the west, so far has He moved our transgressions from us"* **Psalm 103:12(NKJV)**. He has thrown them away. We get angry at Satan because he twists the Word we have grown to love, the Word that guides us, giving us knowledge, understanding, and wisdom. Satan comes to negate that Word. I love, *"in truth and action,"* by my anger at Satan. And I fight if I need to. Our anger is an extension of the heart, rooted in our love for our Lord, and that is fertile ground for truth and action to lash out at Satan. No, we do not respond in emotionalism, but we may get emotional.

The Lord is not talking here about excessive anger, emotionalism. He is talking about righteous anger. Isn't it about time that we get emotional about what darkness is doing to our country, our family, our children, and to us? If we allow Satan to go unchecked, the slogan, "In God, we trust," will not be on our coins, seen on the walls of our legislative halls, let alone written on our children and grandchildren's hearts. How did David physically approach Goliath? He did so aggressively and with anger! Yes, we are lambs and servants in the natural but lions and warriors in the spiritual. Did David have any mercy on Goliath? NO! Did Jesus delay when speaking the Word of the Lord back to Satan? No! Nor should you and I in our wilderness experiences when Satan comes to steal, kill, and destroy our very identity, and everything else we possess in Christ the Messiah!

I have discovered in my three wilderness experiences that

Satan is aggressive and comes with hate to destroy, literally. I, therefore, have found that toward Satan, I must be aggressive and come with emotion when it wells up within me. He is ruthless in attempts to dethrone Christ in your life, in your children's lives, and the lives of every believer on this planet. It is up to the church to convince him otherwise. How did David physically approach Goliath? He did so aggressively and with anger.

It is not the act of getting emotional that brings power to the church. It has everything to do with the feelings within. We speak out because of love, not with emotionalism. Darkness comes at us and ours, and we respond because of the love our Lord has given us for them. I love in truth and action in the natural, like a lamb and servant. I love in truth and action by lashing out at the darkness in the Spirit, like a warrior. Because of my anger at Satan's attempts to harm me and mine, I step out with the Sword of the Spirit. Look at David's words when he responded to Goliath's rantings. **I Samuel 17:45-46(NKJV)**, *"I come against you in the name of the Lord of hosts, the God of the armies of Israel, whom you have defied. The whole world will know that there is a God in Israel. This day the Lord will deliver you into my hand, and I will strike you and take your head from you. And this day I will give the carcasses of the camp of the Philistines to the birds of the air and the wild beasts of the earth, that all the earth may know that there is a God in Israel."* Those are not the words of an idol man. Those are words of a man passionately invested in the identity and authority being challenged and threatened by Goliath.

There was a very traumatic scenario in my life many years ago. People I trust said there was a generational curse in my ancestry. The conclusion made being an only child, and being rooted in the Lord, the demonic in my parent was unable to come down the bloodline to me.

The result was that torment in this person was genuine. With this understanding as a foundation, the Lord allowed me to see the following. I envisioned a ladder inside a house. The base was solidly placed on the first floor, extending to and leaning on the balcony's rail, a floor higher. I envisioned a spirit, a generational curse, in the form of a demon, on the ladder trying to climb down to me. Of course, the Lord prevented it from doing so. In this picture, the Lord helped me understand that if that demon can attempt to come down the ladder to challenge me, I can climb up the ladder to challenge it. One can climb a ladder in two directions. That was the answer! I did not have to watch the hand of darkness torment anymore. I understood the Lord's intentions to climb that ladder, engage in necessary spiritual warfare, and free my parent from the darkness that had entangled life. He was instructing me to declare Jesus Christ, the Father, and the Holy Spirit as Lord over insanity. Be aggressive! Respond to Satan by engaging while on the offense. *My Wilderness Experience* found elsewhere in this book elaborates more on this scenario to the glory and power of our God.

Yes, church! We must run to the battle line! Know that our Lord is capable and willing to stand with us to be aggressive, to come with emotion, fueled with righteous anger to attack the one who comes against us and ours. Therefore, we must come to steal, kill, and destroy every work Satan and his accomplices present. He leaves us no choice. With darkness advancing, the church cannot be idle. Understand there is no middle ground. Let us know we cannot be hesitant regarding the advance of darkness as he wells up his ugly head against the principles and the people of our Lord Jesus Christ in our world today.

CHAPTER 26

Without Mercy, Without Compassion, Without Remorse

The *Merriam-Webster Dictionary* defines the word warrior as, "A person engaged or experienced in warfare: broadly: a person engaged in conflict." Have any of you been engaged in conflict lately? As a person in the wilderness, engaging in battle, you are the very definition of a warrior. **Romans 8:37(NKJV)** says, "*Yet in all these things we are more than conquerors through Him who loved us.*" Church, we need to act like conquerors as darkness tries to overpower us in our wilderness walk, attempting to bring us to the point of unbelief.

There is a miniseries called *Band of Brothers.* It is a story about American 101st Air Born in World War II. In this series, there was an officer named Lieutenant Spiers. His fellow soldiers know him as being a ruthless and heartless soldier. There is a scene in this movie where approximately twenty captured German soldiers are held at gunpoint in a small field by several American soldiers. As Lieutenant Spiers walks down the road next to the field, he walks over to the captured soldiers, offers them each a cigarette, pulls out his lighter, and lights each one. Then, standing several feet away from the group, he turns and sprays the group with his machine gun, killing each one.

Later in the series, Lieutenant Spiers describes a warrior as being without mercy, without compassion, and without remorse." This attitude also should be the heart of a warrior against Satan. Jesus came to destroy the works of the devil without mercy, without compassion, and without remorse. That is the heart of the Lion of Judah against the darkness. That is the heart of Jesus against Satan! How do we spiritually approach Satan as a warrior? The same way David did, and the same way Jesus did, with righteous anger. We should be without mercy, without compassion, without remorse, and most importantly, we should use the Word of God. **John 10:10(NKJV)** says, *"The thief does not come except to steal, and to kill, and to destroy."* That is not a statement to be taken lightly. But understand Satan only influences our territory if we legally give it to him. He is out to steal from you, kill you and yours, and destroy all you have in Christ. Doesn't that make you just a little angry? Do you have children or grandchildren? You may be the only defense on this earth to keep Satan from those you love. You are a person in Christ. You have done well. Know you are a threat to him.

Unfortunately, too many in the church are ill-prepared for the darkness presenting itself in our lives and world. Take on the identity of a warrior that cuts, slashes, severs, and destroys darkness with the Sword of the Spirit. Yes, we become, like Jesus, lambs and servants in the natural in this world, but also like Jesus, we are to become Lions of Judah in the spiritual! If not already established, it is time you learn to become a warrior as well and run to the battle line that Satan has drawn for you. The Lord calls us to be on the offensive to cut off the serpent's head without mercy, without compassion, and without remorse!

CHAPTER 27

Beware of the Power of Fear

Without exception, fear was the most debilitating tool Satan used in my wilderness experiences. At one point in my life, the power of fear overwhelmed me so that I was mentally disabled. I was so involved that I was unable to make fundamental decisions at my business. The power of fear enveloped me, forcing me to bring routine management questions home to get assistance from my wife. There were times I simply could not function. After another incident, a friend gave me cards with scriptures about fear printed on each. As I felt overwhelmed, the only thing that would reverse my fear was reading these verses and speaking the Word to that fear. At times, I had to repeat it every several minutes. Over time it was the Word of God spoken to that fear that broke the cycle.

II Timothy 1:7(NKJV), *"For God has not given us a spirit of fear, but of power and of love and of a sound mind."* Satan came with betrayal in his mind to defuse the love of the Father that was evident in Jesus' mind. Jesus overcame this by speaking the Word without fear. We can cast out fear by attacking aggressively in faith with a sound mind. It is your destiny to walk in this as a child of God.

The result of Jesus' identity was receiving authority from

the Father. The result of authority from the Father was the Holy Spirit's power. The result of the Holy Spirit's power was Satan leaving the wilderness in shame. The wilderness is the first time that Jesus exhibited power. He indeed spoke the Word with a sound mind. He had no fear!

CHAPTER 28

Qualifying for Greatness

The power of the Holy Spirit does not come because we proclaim Christ...only. It comes as we identify with Him in our wilderness. Because of His example, we can go forward now with that power and walk-in nothing less than anointing from the Holy Spirit Himself. *Dictionary.com* defines the word anointing, 1. "to consecrate or make sacred, 2. To dedicate to the service of God". Jesus received His anointing by choosing the Father. In dedicating himself to the service of the Father and by enduring the wilderness without wavering in a challenging place, the Father knew He could trust Jesus. Jesus was qualified for greatness in the process of obtaining the trust of the Father. The same applies to you. By successfully managing your trials and temptations, you can be qualified for greatness in the Lord! It is in the wilderness where He determines if He can trust you.

TGIF Today God Is First Volume 1 by Os Hillman
Monday, June 01 2015

"He trains my hands for battle; my arms can bend a bow of bronze." - **2 Samuel 22:35(NIV)**

Mr. Hillman elaborates by describing David as a man who was a mighty warrior, and that God described him as a man after His own heart. He says that since God chose him as a king at a young age, God took David through his wilderness experience as a "training ground that could be looked on as cruel and unusual punishment by many a person." David had many trials as a fugitive for years. There were family issues and many relationship problems, filling him with highs and lows. He made mistakes because he was human like all of us. Mr. Hillman says, "This was David's training ground; it made the man. Without these hardships, it is doubtful David would have accomplished what he did."

Where did David get his training for battle? Where did it look like cruel and unusual punishment? Where did he have uprisings in his own family? Where did he have relationship problems? Where was his training ground? All were in his wilderness experiences.

Having the Father's authority, you are "NOW QUALIFIED. You, the church, can now have that same authority with opportunity for the same power released in your own life. You, the church, can now be qualified, just like Jesus! **Acts 26:17-18(NIV)**, *"I will rescue you from your own people and from the Gentiles. I am sending you to them."* Why? It is because you are qualified, *"to open their eyes and turn them from darkness to light, and from the power of Satan to (the Power of) God, so that they may receive forgiveness of sins and a place among those who are sanctified by faith in me."* *Merriam-Webster's* dictionary defines sanctified, "to set apart to a sacred purpose or to religious use." That is you!

What is that special purpose? It is to be sent, just like Jesus! Is that your legacy to be sanctified? It is if you choose to identify yourself as a son or a daughter, AND WALK IN IT! **Colossians 1:11-12(NIV)**, *being strengthened with all power according to his glorious might so that,"* (**Who**), *"you may have great endurance and patience, and,"* (**You**), *"giving joyful thanks to the Father, who has,"* (**What**), *"qualified you,"* to (do **What**), *"share in the* *inheritance of his holy people in the kingdom of light."* And what is that inheritance? Anything that is reaped by identity, authority, power, and anointing, to be sent. We have to understand it, choose to walk in it, and act upon it, as Lambs of God and even Lions of Judah. You are in preparation for greatness!

Warrior Power
"WITH MY WEAPONS YOU WILL DESTROY STRONGHOLDS

You are My mighty warriors. You are living on the earth, but you do not fight your battles with the weapons of this world. Instead, you use My power, which can destroy any fortresses of evil. You have been trained for war and equipped with My weapons so that you can destroy the evil imaginations of this world and every bit of worldly knowledge that would keep people from obeying Me. In My strength, you will break through all the enemy's walls and reduce his strongholds to ruins. You will turn back his sword, put an end to his splendor, and cast his throne to the ground. We will cut off nations and demolish their strongholds. Their streets will be left deserted, and no one will pass through their land."

2 Corinthians 10:3-5(NASB)
For though we walk in the flesh, we do not war according to the flesh, for the weapons of our warfare are not of the flesh, but divinely powerful for the destruction of fortresses. We are destroying speculations and every lofty thing raised up against the knowledge of God, and we are taking every thought captive to the obedience of Christ."

Psalm 89:40 (NASB)
You have broken down all his walls; You have brought his strongholds to ruin.

Psalm 89:43-44 (NASB) *You also turn back the edge of his sword And have not made him stand in battle. You have made his splendor to cease And cast his throne to the ground.*

Prayer Declaration

Deliver me from my strong enemy, from them that are too strong for me. I am Your battle-ax and weapon of war. I am Your anointed, and You give me great deliverance. I am Your End Time warrior. Use me as Your weapon against the enemy.

From *Daily Declarations for Spiritual Warfare* by John Eckhardt, page 65."

Wednesday Wisdom
Dr. Mike Murdock
Secrets of the uncommon Life

Dr. Murdock says that what we are willing to overcome brings us an uncommon life. He tells us that an uncommon life is not without mistakes and that all of us fail at times. *"All have sinned and come short of the glory of God."* **Romans 3:23(NKJV)** *"For a righteous man may fall seven times and rise again.'* **Proverbs 24:16(NKJV)** In a most profound truth, he says that we all fall, but it is the great ones that get up. "The Uncommon Life is simply a life of victory after chaos...order after confusion." He indicates it is a life of battle, of winning. "Champions are willing to do things they hate to create something else they love. Champions are willing to walk away from something they desire to protect something they love. "A champion makes decisions that create the future they desire."

You are a champion! You are a warrior! In Christ, you have an uncommon life coming through the wilderness.

CHAPTER 29

Ready, Aim, Fire

You may recall that a subtheme of *Road Map Through the Wilderness* is that the Lord desires us to see ourselves through His eyes rather than seeing ourselves through our own eyes. That is understanding His identity of us rather than our own. An interesting slant on that theme demonstrates how Satan sees us. How exactly does he view the Christian? In my young adulthood, I, like many of my male peers, was drafted into the military. Initially, precluding all service activity in the military is the dreaded basic training. There were three segments to our training there. Before reporting for training, however, to formalize our obligation, all had to take an oath. We declared our intentions by vocalizing our commitment to our country. Arriving at the military base, they processed us through the receiving area. They performed numerous medical tests, a dental examination, shaved our hair, issued clothing, and other innumerable requirements preparing us for two weeks for the basic training activity.

In **Phase I,** we started calisthenics, were given instructions on how to march, make our bed, salute an officer, and other general activities conducted day to day. In **Phase II,** we learned how to handle our weapon on the parade ground, break down, and clean our rifle. In **Phase III,** at the rifle range, ultimately, we received hands-on application learning to shoot our weapon at the rifle range and techniques on hand-to-hand combat. They planned each area carefully to enable us to learn skills to become soldiers, a warrior ultimately. Each phase had a unique purpose. Each in succession brought the trainee closer to becoming a capable warrior enabling the trainee to graduate, prepared for battle.

Above, basic training stated can be compared to our wilderness walk. The Lord is preparing you and me to be spiritual warriors. The equivalent to taking an oath is our salvation experience. Although we may not feel like it, by inviting Jesus into our lives, by coming into the kingdom of God, we have signed up ultimately to become a spiritual warrior. Arriving at the receiving station, we are issued kingdom clothes, our identity, and issued our weapon, the Word of God. In **Phase I,** we start basic training by attending church and Bible classes, growing in His Word, learning how to pray, and other general skills we need to conduct our day to day activities. In **Phase II**, we are learning more of the Word, how it applies to our own and other's lives, and how to appropriate the weapons and tools the Lord has given us. In **Phase III**, we learn the advanced skills of a warrior, how to wrestle with principalities and powers in hand to hand combat and how to use our weapon, the Sword of the Spirit, with accuracy and effectiveness. Ultimately coming out of our basic training, we have experience in using the Word effectively as weaponry for kingdom victory.

I envisioned basic training as a noble event, ultimately enabling me to eliminate an enemy of my own, my family, my country, and my Lord. How, then, might Satan see this process about his interests? The above process is described in an old narrative, "Ready, Aim, Fire." In **Phase I,** he sees a recruit for Jesus. He sees a potential threat, but he is on the alert, getting **ready**. In **Phase II**, he considers that threat increasing as practical training develops the new Christian in Word and deed, growing in training strategies used in spiritual warfare, **Aim**. And in **Phase III**, Satan sees the warrior fully prepared, using a weapon with proficiency, ready to move out of training and into full battle, **Fire**. From the time of salvation until you exit, the wilderness is a preparation to develop a warrior's identity in you. You are given warrior power by exiting the wilderness, and Satan knows it. Each step potentially prepares the Christian for spiritual warfare. Each phase brings the Christian closer to becoming a competent warrior, skilled when confronted by the enemy of your soul. Satan's deceptive attempts are subtly maneuvered to disarm you in your most challenging place, the wilderness. Obtain our Lord's knowledge, His Spirit, and His authority preparing yourself for battle, for your King awaits on the throne to lead you to victory.

Run to the Battle Line! There is a war going on!

CHAPTER 30

So, What's the Point?

I. Jesus did not exhibit authority to humanity until after His wilderness victory. **Mark 1:22(NASB)**, *"They were amazed at His teaching; for He was teaching them as one having authority, and not as the scribes."* **Mark 1:27(NASB)**, *"They were all amazed, so that they debated among themselves, saying, 'What is this? A new teaching with authority! He commands even the unclean spirits, and they obey Him.'* **Luke 4:32(NASB)**, *"and they were amazed at His teaching, for His message was with authority."* **Luke 5:24(NASB)**, *"But, so that you may know that the Son of Man has authority on earth to forgive sins,"* He said to the paralytic, *"I say to you, get up, and pick up your stretcher and go home."* Nothing happened in Jesus' ministry until after His wilderness walk. He had to go through and master the seven steps to come out in power.

The wilderness was mandated so Jesus could begin His ministry with the authority of the Father. To be sent, the wilderness is also mandated for you and me to walk in power and anointing as well. The same process is available to us with the very same results. Can anyone person accomplish all that Jesus accomplished? The answer is a definite no. We are not a bunch of little God's running around. But since we all are a part of the body of Christ, and since Jesus is the perfect human, that part that we represent can have nothing less than full anointing. Because of that, it is my opinion that everyone is a ten at something in God's kingdom.

Years ago, a family came to our church and ministered in music. Seated in the front row was a young man, their son, who obviously had down syndrome. My heart went out to him as he sat there with no others sitting near him. It was obvious to me that they placed him there to keep a close eye on him throughout the service. Nearing the end of their ministry time, his mother walked to the front row where he was seated and assisted him in standing up. Helping him walk forward, she led him to the piano bench, sat him down, and positioned the bench, giving the appearance that he was going to play. After a brief introduction, this young man filled the hall, and this musician's spirit, with the most beautiful music imaginable. In my four years as a music major, I sat through many piano recitals presented by accomplished pianists but never heard anything like the anointing of this young man. Miraculously, he was a ten out of ten, batting 1,000, untrained, he never had a music lesson in his life. I saw a young man who could do very little for himself, playing the piano bringing supernatural, heavenly music to the worship service. In my astonishment, he was fulfilling what the Father created him to be.

With the Father's authority received in the wilderness, you can fulfill what He has created you to be. By His example, Jesus has shown us precisely how to grab hold of that authority. It was in the wilderness. Yes, our experiences are at least unpleasant, none the less, planned by God. That is because it is His agenda for us not only to obtain His authority but to exhibit it through us. It is accomplished by you and me placing our identity in and as a son or daughter of God. We achieve that by placing our identity as the Lord's, by acting on it and speaking the Word back to Satan, thus, not only receiving but also walking in the Father's authority. Therefore, Jesus was *authorized.* As sons and brothers, as daughters and sisters, you too can be *authorized*! **Romans 8:29(NKJV)**, *"Jesus the first of many brethren."* Therefore, several questions arise.

1. Are we recognizing and receiving authority in our wilderness walk, or are we going in circles as the Israelites did learning nothing for forty years in their wilderness experience? Are we going to mirror the same fate as they?
2. If we have received the Father's authority and are walking in it, do we exercise that authority? Are we applying it to the lives of others as well, like Jesus? Authority held within is of no consequence it becomes authority going out. **So, What's the Point – Let us understand that your wilderness experience is a walk not only planned by God but ordained by God to receive and implement His authority in lives, resulting in nothing less than full anointing. Authority withheld and not implemented to advance God's Kingdom is of little significance.**

II. It is choosing identity in the Father that releases authority to you. It is speaking the Word to darkness with authority that releases God's power against the opposition. It is only the Lord's power that can destroy the works of the devil. Learning these truths in the wilderness enables you to stand on the battlefield against the biggest, ugliest, and worst that Satan can throw at you without effect. Engaging against darkness is our call to destroy the works of the devil as Jesus did. Like David, we run to the battle line and engage. Like Jesus, we are the aggressor with the Sword of the Spirit and engage, that is an attack, not against flesh and blood, but at principalities, powers, and rulers of darkness.

So, What's the Point - Placing our identity in the Lord and

ACTING on it as Jesus did releases the Father's authority by the spoken Word to darkness, unto real Holy Spirit POWER.

III. Jesus had not eaten for forty days. He was starving. Malnutrition causes fatigue and weakness. It affects & causes loss of essential body functions. Clarity of thought can be compromised. It can cause headaches, dizziness, low blood pressure, and low blood sugar.

All the experiences that affected Jesus when he was hungry affect us. Our physical body is no different than His. He is one hundred percent human, just like you and me. Satan is an opportunist. He knows when to arrive at your weakest point. Expect it. Be prepared for Him. When it happens, do not be surprised. Do not be concerned about your wellbeing. Do not look at the circumstances. Do not look at the giant in Goliath proportions standing before you. Look at your Lord. Speak the Word of God into your opposition! You are informed and ready now, prepared with knowledge and understanding, so continue to move forward, praying for wisdom to deal with Satan's attacks.

So, What's the Point – Satan is an opportunist. It is the wounded animal that attracts the predator. He will approach us when we are weak. But now informed, we can be prepared and ready, equipped with the knowlege and understanding to stand against the wiles of the devil.

IV. The Jewish nation stayed in the wilderness for forty years, and that generation never entered the Promised Land except for Joshua and Caleb. The direct route only took several weeks to travel. Because they placed their identity in Satan rather than the triune God, they circled in the wilderness and never did come out. Decide to put your identity in the Lord immediately. Receive the Father's authority quickly. Decide to act on it promptly. Speak the Word directly to darkness in haste. **James 4:7(NASB),** "*Submit* *therefore to God. Resist the devil, and he will flee from you"* ...and do it now! The sooner we start the sooner darkness weakens. The sooner darkness weakens, the faster the fight is over, and we may walk out of the wilderness earlier.

So, What's the Point? – Run to the battle line and engage quickly. The length of your stay may depend on you.

V. In *Dictionary.com*, the word react is defined "to respond to a stimulus in a particular manner." For our conversation, that stimulus is trials and temptations. It involves a lack of thought or intellectual application. In our case, it is a lack of Biblical application. It is a knee jerk reaction on our part. Misguided emotions can result in sin in our wilderness situation, especially when we react without thought. That is what Satan wants. The *Mirriam Webster Dictionary* defines the word respond as, "something constituting a reply or reaction." A reply is based on an evaluation, or thought, or intellectual application. A reaction is simply action without thought.

We can be tempted with sin when we are experiencing the wilderness. Learn by Jesus' example in your thought process in the wilderness. We do not have to react with negative emotions, bitterness, or sin in any way. Be careful not to react when presented with trials and temptations. Respond with intellectual application based on prayer and the Word of God.

So, What's the Point – Respond with prayer, and thought. Do not react with sin to Satan's temptations in the wilderness.

VI. Decisions determine our future. Decisions affect our witness. Decisions affect the timing of our ministry. Decisions determine the effectiveness of our ministry. Decisions in the wilderness are crucial. I have experienced the effects of wrong choices made in my wilderness walks and have paid a dear price. On the other hand, decisions made using our Lord's example enables us to come out of our wilderness authorized in Holy Spirit power as victors instead of victims. The devil wants our bodies scattered throughout the desert, just like the Jewish nation, dead. The Lord wants us to come out in power, anointed, and sent. That is the difference in decision making, and that is a big deal!

So, What's the Point - Do not minimize the decisions in your wilderness walk and life.

VII. Take David's lead. Take Jesus' lead! Speak out to darkness. State truth, the Word of God. State precisely a Word that applies to the scenario before you. State the Word in faith. Apply the black snake story. Be on the offense. It takes an aggressor to cut off the head of the serpent. You must be an aggressor in the wilderness to win the battle. You cannot display power when you are defending yourself. You can succeed, however, with aggression against the darkness.

So, What's the Point? Be the aggressor and speak the Word. To the enemy, be ferocious with righteous anger, and mean it.

VIII. A. Related- Think of the bonding nature of kinship in the natural. In our history lessons, we learn of the clans in Scotland. Each person has their own identity with the others in the clan. The family's identity is so strong that each group has its unique design of plaid clothing, all because they are related. Although I cannot endorse the actions of the Hatfield's and the McCoy's, each member's bond to their family is strong as we see them standing together, each family fighting the other. Every person is a part of the family in kinship. Each has a collective identity rooted in the bloodline, each fighting the other to the death, bonded in the blood.

Think of the bonding nature of kinship in the Lord. Think of the powerful bloodline with Jesus as brother and God as Father.

That bond is no less authentic than the relationship of a natural family. In the natural, kinship creates a bond sealed by the blood. That common ground is the catalyst for that bond. It is intense! Indeed, that bond is so much greater than the natural bond. By seeing the Father giving His son unto death to create that bond, it is solidified seeing the Father giving His son unto death to create that bond. It is not by natural bloodlines but by Jesus' shed blood. We walk in true authentic identity as sons/daughters of the Father and brothers/ sisters of the Christ. We establish identity and receive authority in the wilderness experience because we are in a relationship as family with Jesus. It is the Lord who unleashes the power of that bond. It all happens when we choose to place our identity in the Lord, most high God. We are related to Jesus and the Father.

B. Relationship - II Corinthians 5:21(AMPC), *"For our sake He made Christ (virtually) to be sin, who knew no sin, so that in and through Him we might become (endued with, viewed as in, and examples of) the righteousness of God (what we ought to be, approved and, acceptable and in right relationship with Him, by His goodness)."* We are a relative to our Lord Christ as brother/sister, and to the Father as son/daughter. Therefore, we have a unique relationship.

C. To Know - Philippians 3:10-11(NKJV), *"that I may know Christ and the power of His resurrection and the fellowship of sharing in His sufferings, being conformed to His death, if by any means I may attain to the resurrection from the dead."*

Os Hillman, states this is Paul's mission statement in *TGIF Today God Is First Volume 1*. He speaks of three objectives here. 1." to know Christ, 2. to know the power of His resurrection, 3. to know the fellowship of sharing in His sufferings." He says everything that "flows from these three objectives becomes a by-product (result)." Salvation is a bi-product of knowing Him. Knowing the power resulting from His resurrection in miracles, becomes a by-product. Christ's likeness is a bi-product of knowing the fellowship of sharing His sufferings. The magnitude, the strength of God's power, is based on knowing Him. Our power comes from the Father's authority received in the wilderness. The strength of Holy Spirit power that you can display results from your ongoing relationship with Him. Knowing Him depends on the relationship.

We are looking at the interaction of two words here, being related, and having a relationship. Being related has to do with the bloodline. The relationship has to do with an interaction with the person Jesus. That is what separates Christianity from other religions. Our relatives are kin to us; thus, we share in a bloodline. We are, therefore, related to one another. **Romans 8:29(NKJV)** says that *"Jesus is the first of many brethren."* We are brethren. And in that, we share the bond of kinship. We are related. But we are also in a relationship.

Let us understand the bond of kinship, the strength of family, the strength of Jesus' blood, and how the Lord sees it. It is a birthright! That is a powerful truth, church! We can now understand the significance of knowing who we have become in His blood (related), and that relationship to the King of Kings is our birthright. In Jesus, we are not invited to the dinner table as guests. Because we belong, because we are loved, and because we are legitimately kin, we are invited as family members. Not only as a family member but invited to the dinner table as His bride! We belong there, because we are loved, and because we are legitimately kin. Understand, in the family, we are accepted, as family.

So, What's the Point? – In our Lord, we are related, but we also have a relationship! With the bond of kinship and strength through relationship, the Lord gives us an opportunity unique to Christ's body of believers. Being related comes from our birthright. James 4:8(NASB), *"Draw near to God and He will*

draw near to you." **Being related, we receive power coming out of the wilderness. But the magnitude of that power is determined by how well we establish our relationship with Him! Kinship offers power coming into us. Relationship determines the strength of that power coming out of us. The closer we get, the more power we receive.**

IX. Satan came at Jesus not once, not twice but three times. Each time he came in a unique way, totally different. And it was not until the third attempt that Satan finally left Jesus' presence. The Word says Satan tempted Jesus in every way we are. By being there forty days, I have considered it possible that Satan tempted Him more than three times. Perhaps the Lord summarizes numerous temptations in these three mentioned in scripture. I do not know. However, if Satan had within himself the rebellion, treachery, and hatred to destroy Jesus' identity as Son of the Father, and considering that at least three times Satan tempted Him, why would I think Satan will leave me the first time I resist him?

As I think back at my failed attempts to resist, there were times when I wondered why he was still there. Being prepared for battle in these wilderness struggles, I said the appropriate scriptures. When Satan was still there after the first attempt, my thought was, "Well, that did not work. It must not be God's will" and walk away from the fight. Too many times, I have missed God's best by giving up too soon.

The obvious question that we need to ask here is, "How many times do I have to resist before he leaves me?" The answer is easy, as many times as it takes. **James 4:7(NASB)** says, *"Submit therefore to God. Resist the devil, and he will flee from you."* Do not quit until he leaves. He must go! He has no choice! The Word says it. He has no power to overcome the Word! Convince him of that. Convince him that you know that. When he leaves does not matter. That is up to God. What matters is that we resist until he goes. Understand that to resist is not necessarily a single event. If we submit and resist, he will go!

So, What's the Point - If Satan was so arrogant to come after Jesus at least three times, what makes me think he will always leave after the first time I resist? If we resist and continue to resist, he will flee!

X. If we understand identity and understand the strength of bonding, the power of sharing a bloodline with our most high God, and if we know the authority that comes with it, what do we have to fear? Too often, I have found myself in wilderness situations, dealing with anxiety, exhibiting an attitude of hopelessness, experiencing deep duress, coming to the point of despair, and walking in the Poor Me Syndrome. **II Timothy 1:7(NKJV)** says, *"For God has not given us a spirit of fear, but of power and of love, and of a sound mind"*. If the Father did not, then who did? Remember that Satan is trying to get us to an attitude of unbelief. Jesus had no fear in the wilderness. He was not the victim. David expressed no fear when he ran to the battle line. Satan is always the author of your fear.

Revelation 5:4-6(NASB), " *Then I began to weep greatly because no one was found worthy to open the [a]book or to look into it; and one of the elders said to me, 'Stop weeping; behold, the Lion that is from the tribe of Judah, the Root of David, has overcome so as to open the [b]book and its seven seals.' And I saw [c]between the throne (with the four living creatures) and the elders ....a Lamb standing, as if slain...* The Lion of Judah is found worthy, but He saw a Lamb standing as if slain. They are the same; the Lion and the Lamb referenced are both Jesus!!!

Over the years, I have not heard much from the pulpit about the heart of a Lion. What about the Lion? In knowing who we are and whose we are, by example, we can go through the wilderness exhibiting the fierceness as Jesus lashing out at Satan, as David did, having run to the battle line to Goliath. Jesus is the Lamb of God in the natural, but He is the Lion of Judah in the spiritual. **James 1: 2-4(NASB)**, *"Consider it all joy, my brethren, when you encounter various trials, knowing that the testing of your faith produces endurance. And let endurance have its perfect result,"* **Why?** *"so that you may be perfect and complete, lacking in nothing."*

The following is a quote from one of my devotionals, *Daily Declarations for Spiritual Warfare*, by John Eckhardt.

"YOU WILL PURSUE YOUR ENEMIES AND OVERTAKE THEM

My precious child, you do not need to be filled with terror and fear when your enemies plot against you and pursue you. Trust instead in Me, for indeed I am Your God, and your times are indeed in My hands. In the shelter of My presence you are hidden from your enemies and from the intrigues of evil men. Do not be afraid of your enemies. I have given them into your hand. Not one of them will be able to withstand you. But don't stop—pursue your enemies. Attack them from the rear, for I, the Lord your God, have given them into your hand. I will remove your enemies from your land just as I would remove savage beasts, and the sword will not pass through your country."

Psalm 31:14-15(NASB)
*"**14** But as for me, I trust in You, O Lord, I say, "You are my God." My times are in Your hand; Deliver me from the hand of my enemies and from those who persecute me".*

Psalm 31:20(NASB) *You hide them in the secret place of Your*

presence from the conspiracies of man; You keep them secretly in a [a] shelter from the strife of tongues.

Joshua 10:8(NASB) *The Lord said to Joshua, "Do not fear them, for I have given them into your hands; not [a]one of them shall stand before you."*

Joshua 10:19(NASB) *"but do not stay there yourselves; pursue your enemies and [a]attack them in the rear. Do not allow them to enter their cities, for the Lord your God has delivered them into your hand."*

Leviticus 26:6-8(NASB)

"I shall also grant peace in the land, so that you may lie down with no one making you tremble. I shall also eliminate harmful beasts from the land, and no sword will pass through your land. But you will chase your enemies and they will fall before you by the sword; five of you will chase a hundred, and a hundred of you will chase ten thousand, and your enemies will fall before you by the sword".

Prayer Declaration

I trust you, Lord. I celebrate and shout because You are kind. You saw all my suffering, and You cared for me. You kept me from the hands of my enemies, and You set me free. I will praise You, Lord, for showing great kindness when I was like a city under attack. You answered my prayer when I shouted for help."

So, What's the Point? There is no need to be afraid in the wilderness when you understand, like the one described in Revelations 5, you are also, both a lamb and a lion in Jesus.

XI. In a group meeting, I heard a well-rooted brother stand up and apologize for a wilderness experience he was going through. His explanation illustrated his embarrassment that it was occurring, as if it were his fault, that he was somehow responsible for it or at least allowing it in his life. It was the Holy Spirit that led Jesus into the wilderness. If He chooses, the Holy Spirit will lead you there. Let us remember the Father has an agenda for you in the wilderness. The wilderness is an opportunity to walk in power and anointing as Jesus did. Learn from Jesus' example what to do to determine how to get through it! Being in the wilderness is nothing to be ashamed of. It is not a sign of weakness. It is a sign of being a threat!

So, What's the Point? - Do not be embarrassed. Do not be apologetic about your presence in the wilderness. Do not be ashamed. God has a purpose in the wilderness that you may be fully prepared to be sent.

XII. Years ago, I heard a prophetess proclaim, "Grab Hold! Grab Hold! Grab Hold." Unable to remember the prophecy, those two words are the only words I can recall. They do ring in my ears still. If we "Grab Hold," we are clutching something already in existence, something available. As Christians, we already have the Father's authority available to us. It is simply up to me and you to "Grab Hold" of it. I remember pleading with the Lord to remove the dilemma before me, remove me from my problematic scenario, or otherwise resolve my wilderness dilemma. I can not help but think that at times His response was, No! Do you not understand? I have already done it for you. Just "Grab Hold!"

We have the opportunity to see Satan leave our presence, understanding that his agenda failed. We already have the Father's power available to us. It is only up to you and me to "Grab Hold" of it in the wilderness. In every situation, conversation, scenario, and with every person I meet, I am authorized to do exactly that. "Grab Hold" of His authority, ask for guidance, and respond in power. It could range from a gentle word, an act of kindness, or a declaration to the darkness that he is not welcome and must leave in Jesus' name. The Father has predestined us to conform to the image of Jesus, and in every situation, "Grab Hold!"

So, What's the Point? - Receive what He has already made available to you. Grab Hold of His authority!

XIII. As I think back to my wilderness situations, I remember the times that I did not display the characteristics of a warrior very well. As I pondered, even more, I found myself tired and weak, thus being ineffective, being a victim. If I were truthful with myself, I would have to honestly say that to mount a campaign of war on the enemy was something that I did not want to do. At that time, I did not want to be a warrior. Although I was uncomfortable where I was, the thought of going into battle, the idea of mounting an attack was not pleasing. The thought of staying right where I was in difficulty and misery was better than standing up and running forward aggressively engaging. Even though I was uncomfortable, it was easier to do nothing than making an effort to go into battle. These times, I felt spiritually numb.

We need to make that effort. Yes, the fight can be exhausting. I may get wounded, or I might come face to face with my enemy. I made an unconscious decision to stay in the wilderness rather than stepping up and out to fight.

Being a musician, I had the privilege of presenting a song in ministry named *The Army of the Lord,* written by Lindell Cooley and recorded by the group, Harvest. Some of the words follow.

> "Are we walking into the enemy's camp
> Laying our weapons down
> Shedding our armor as we go
> And leaving it on the ground
> We've got to be strong in the power of His might
> And prove to the enemy

We are the army of the Lord
And we've won the victory"

Battle at times is necessary. I think of Nehemiah working with one hand, building the temple while holding a sword in the other. That was not convenient for him. The battle is not pleasant. It takes effort. It can be exhausting. The beauty is, if we apply God's Word, we are victorious! We are more than a conqueror. Jesus never said it would be easy. He just said it would be worth it!

So, What's the Point - Many of us are not effective warriors in the wilderness because it is easier to stay where we are than to stand up and fight.

XIV. I Corinthians 10:4(NKJV), *"and all drank the same spiritual drink. For they drank of that spiritual Rock that followed them, and that Rock was Christ."* We can see in this reference that the Holy Spirit was not alone in the wilderness. Jesus was accompanying the Jewish nation in their wilderness experience as well. I find it extremely comforting to know that even though I may not sense His presence at times in my deep wilderness struggles, Jesus and all that He is and represents, accompanies me in those most challenging wilderness times. The poem *Footprints in The Sand* comes to mind.

"One night I dreamed a dream. As I was walking along the beach with my Lord, across the dark sky flashed scenes from my life. For each scene, I noticed two sets of footprints in the sand, one belonging to me and one to my Lord.

After the last scene of my life flashed before me, I looked back at the sand's footprints. I noticed that many times along the path of my life, especially at the very lowest and saddest times, there was only one set of footprints.

This troubled me, so I asked the Lord about it. 'Lord, you said once I decided to follow you, you'd walk with me all the way. But

I notice that during the saddest and most troublesome times of my life, there was only one set of footprints. I don't understand why, when I needed you the most, you would leave me.'

He whispered, 'My precious child, I love you and will never leave you. Never, ever, during your trials and tests. When you saw only one set of footprints, it was then I carried you." Author unknown. Thank you, Jesus, for carrying me in my most difficult experiences. Found on *www.onlythebible.com.*

So, What's the point? In my most difficult place, in my time of deepest despair, when I feel alone and abandoned, I am comforted knowing that my Lord is present.

XV. – II Timothy 4:1-5 (NASB), – *"I solemnly charge you in the presence of God and of Christ Jesus, who is to judge the living and the dead, and by His appearing and His kingdom: preach the word; be ready in season and out of season; reprove, rebuke, exhort, with great patience and instruction. For the time will come when they will not endure sound doctrine; but wanting to have their ears tickled, they will accumulate for themselves teachers in accordance to their own desires, and will turn away their ears from the truth and will turn aside to myths. But you, be sober in all things, endure hardship, do the work of an evangelist, fulfill your ministry."*

That is the Point!

CHAPTER 31

Summary

The wilderness is a walk that Jesus walked. We can see His example detailed in our Father's Word. Therefore, we can apply what we learn by His example. By doing so, you can expect the very same results. Satan wants us in the wilderness to bring us to the point of unbelief. He accomplishes that by challenging our identity as authentic kin to the creator of the universe. The Father wants us in the wilderness for a limited time to experience the same process with a much different result; to come out prepared and authorized to be sent. We have determined Jesus went in the wilderness filled with the Holy Spirit, but He came out of the wilderness with the power of the Holy Spirit. Something happened in there!

Jesus has shown us seven steps in the road through the wilderness.

1. Jesus heard the **Father's Words** while on the bank of the river; His identity.

2. Jesus heard **opposition** from Satan, disclaiming the Father's Words.

3. Jesus had to **think** about the two scenarios presented before Him.

4. Jesus had to **choose** with whom he was going to identify.

5. Jesus **submitted** to God and made the Father His Lord.

6. Jesus received the Father's **authority**.

7. Jesus placed identity and authority into action. He **engaged** by resisting the devil's trials and temptations.

That is the process for Jesus in the wilderness. That is the process for you in the wilderness as well. That is His road. That is your Road Map. The amazing opportunity He has given you is to locate yourself at any given place on this road, follow and implement by Jesus' example and come out of the wilderness. The length of stay may depend on you. The incredible truth is that you can come out in the Holy Spirit's power as well, just like Jesus. Whether your ministry is Holy Spirit ministry or custodial ministry, each is as significant as the other. You can come out of your wilderness trials and tribulations anointed.

An amazing discovery about this walk through the wilderness is that each step achieved on this road is dependent upon the previous. Until one accomplishes the previous step, one cannot move on to the next step. It has an order that simplifies the process, which in turn helps me understand my process. We have determined in **Isaiah 61** that the Father sent the Messiah to fulfill what He created Jesus to be beyond the wilderness. Therefore, like Jesus, to fulfill what the Father created us to be, in Christ, we can also be sent. Let us consider that;

To be **sent**, I need an anointing.

To be anointed, I must **engage** and exhibit power.

To exhibit power, I must have the Father's **authority**.

To have the Father's authority, I must **submit** to the Father.

To have an identity as son/daughter, I must **choose** Him.

To choose Him, I must give **thought**.

To give thought, I must hear an **opposing word** from Satan.

To hear opposing words from Satan, I must hear **Father's Words** of identity.

Here we can see the pattern in Jesus' walk, which enables us to see the pattern in our life.

Before making my final submission of this book to the publisher, my wife Donna stated this observation in our morning devotion time. "If Christians only knew and used the power and authority that we have available, this would be a different world." In my opinion, this truth is precisely what the Lord says to us in *Road Map Through the Wilderness*. Let us remember that worship places identity. In identity, we receive authority. The one to whom we place identity is the one from whom we receive authority. Placing our identity as the Father's child with submission brings the authority of the Father. The catalyst for that process is worship. With authority received and resistance applied, power goes forth with the devil fleeing referenced in **James 4:7**. Be a doer. Initiate the Word of God in your occurrences with Satan. We need not take on the character of a victim, as so many of us have done. Run to the battle line with aggression and cut off the serpent's head, ultimately coming out of the wilderness. Know the Father's will for your life is to be anointed and sent. Understand that the wilderness is preparation for that privilege.

Jesus went into the wilderness filled with the Holy Spirit.
He walked out of the wilderness with the power of the Holy Spirit
Something happened in there. He received authority.

You walk into the wilderness filled with the Holy Spirit.
You walk out of the wilderness with the power of the Holy Spirit.
Something happens in there. You receive authority.
Now you can also bat 1000.

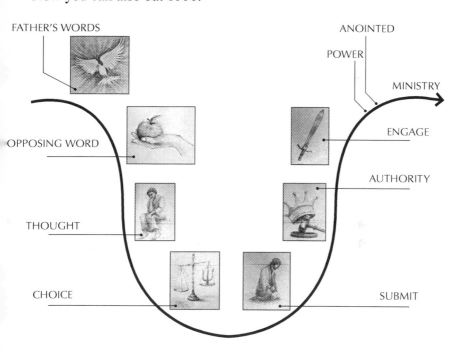

FATHER'S WORDS

ANOINTED

POWER

MINISTRY

ENGAGE

OPPOSING WORD

AUTHORITY

THOUGHT

CHOICE

SUBMIT

CHAPTER **32**

· ·

Examples for Purpose

Understanding the significance of identifying your specific location in the wilderness, we can ask this question. What purpose does the wilderness serve? Mentioned earlier, it merely enables you to determine your location and complete our Lord's agenda in the wilderness. It is a tool, an opportunity, for you to recognize and avoid the fruits Satan desires in your trials and temptations. That sin is his agenda. We can avoid specifically what the Jewish nation succumbed to in their forty years of struggle and move into anointed ministry, healed, delivered, and qualified.

I Corinthians 10:6-11(NKJV) helps us understand, in detail, what the Jewish nation's struggle was in the wilderness. It helps us understand our battle is in the wilderness. *"Now these things became our examples, to the intent that we should not lust after the things of evil as they also lusted. And do not become idolaters as were some of them. As it is written, "The people sat down to eat and drink, and rose up to play." Nor let us commit sexual immorality, as some of them did, and in one day twenty three thousand fell; nor let us tempt Christ, as some of them also tempted, and were destroyed by serpents; nor complain, as some of them complained, and were destroyed by the destroyer. Now all* *these things happened to them as examples, and they were written for our admonition, upon whom the ends of the ages have come."*

Let us not overlook this most profound statement in the last sentence. Is the Lord telling us, telling you, the Jewish experience is precisely an example for you today? Is it possible the wilderness walk the Jewish nation experienced is an example for all but specifically for our generation? Is it possible the time before us today is a time for us, the church, to understand the truths in the message in this scripture above? Should we consider that our Lord is demonstrating these wilderness events for you and me as an example for our purpose today? Can we say we are those to whom the end of this age has come? **II Timothy 3:1-5(NKJV)** says, *"but know this, that in the last days perilous times will come: For men will be lovers of themselves, lovers of money, boasters, proud, blasphemers, disobedient to parents, unfaithful, unholy, unloving, unforgiving, slanderers, without self-control, brutal, despisers of good, traders, headstrong, haughty, lovers of pleasure rather than lovers of God, having a form of godliness but denying its power."*

I cannot deny the changes in humanity's behavior evolving over my lifetime to resemble this scripture. However, we are cautioned not to anticipate the end of this age; specifically, Jesus' second coming. Jesus said in **Matthew 25:13 (NKJV)**, *"Watch therefore for you know neither the day nor the hour in which the Son of Man is coming."* Our Lord does, however, give us hints of activity before the last days. **Luke 21:7-11(NKJV)** *"So they asked Him, saying, 'Teacher, but when will these things be? And what sign will there be when these things are about to take place?'*

And He said: 'Take heed that you not be deceived. For many will come in My name, saying, 'I am He,' and, 'The time has drawn near.' [d]Therefore do not [e]go after them. But when you hear of wars and commotions, do not be terrified; for these things must come to pass first, but the end will not come immediately. And He said to them, 'Nation will rise against nation, and kingdom against kingdom. And there will be great earthquakes in various places, and famines and pestilences; and there will be fearful sights and great signs from heaven."

It is not my intention to say when or if the end of this age is upon us. I am not a prophet. Nor do I claim to be a Bible theologian. However, we are in a time that we must consider we are in that season or nearing it. Therefore, we must give serious thought and prayer to the examples the Lord gives us through Israel's failures in the wilderness. How can we avoid their fate? How can we learn from them? If this time is near, let us carefully ponder and seek God for the importance of these examples for us today. It does not appear to be a coincidence that our Lord is sharing this message of *Road Map Through the Wilderness* and specifically **I Corinthians 10:6-11** today. If not a coincidence, my question is, why? What is the significance? I can only speculate this is for our admonition to grasp the urgency of **I Corinthians 10:6-11** for this day and the days to come. Is there an urgency to move through the wilderness, for power to be, *"upon whom the ends of the ages have come"* **I Corinthians 10:11(NKJV)**?

Os Hillman helps us understand that ultimately to be sent is the whole purpose of the wilderness unto power and anointing.

The Purpose of the Desert
TGIF Today God Is First Volume 1 by Os Hillman
Wednesday, January 07 2015
*Therefore, behold, I will allure Israel and bring her into the wilderness, and I will speak tenderly to her [to reconcile Israel to me]. - **Hosea 2:14(AMP)***

Mr. Hillman asks, what is the best way to communicate with someone if you are trying to get, "the message through?" Distractions prevent us from giving our undivided attention to the messenger. He tells us that God has a way of doing that to us to get our full attention. As examples, he uses Paul in Arabia for three years, and Moses in the desert for forty years.

He points out that the Lord must direct us and lead us through the desert to accomplish His work in us. He says, "God must take us into the desert to give us the privilege to be used in His Kingdom." By removing the things that hinder us, he makes the point that it is here we change. He says that He uses the desert to accomplish what He wants and then bring us out to fulfill who He created me to be. That happens when we have spent sufficient time for preparation. He makes an excellent point by stating that, "God uses enlarged trials to produce enlarged saints so He can put them in enlarged places!"

"I Corinthians 10:12-13(NKJV) continues saying, *"Therefore, let him who thinks he stands take heed lest he fall. No temptation has overtaken you except such as is common to man; but God is faithful, who will not allow you to be tempted beyond what you are able, but with the temptation will also make the way of escape, that you may be able to bear it."* During extreme difficulty, too many times it seems impossible to think relief is available. But the Lord has all things under control. He loves you! Considering the one thing we most fear might seem inevitable, He says in **Joshua 1:5(NKJV)**, *"I will not leave you nor forsake you."*

I have experienced three horrific wilderness experiences, and more. Each time, without exception, I received that relief, along with restoration received. The Lord provided a way of escape. **Psalm 37:23-26(NKJV)**, *"The steps of a good man are ordered by the Lord, and He delights in his way. Though he fall, he shall not be utterly cast down; for the Lord upholds him with His hand. I have been young, and now am old; yet I have not seen the righteous forsaken, nor his descendants begging bread."*

Luke 4:14(NKJV), *"Now when the devil had ended every temptation, he departed from Him until an opportune time."* There is an end. It will stop. **Joshua 1:5b(NKJV)** says, *"I will not leave you or forsake you."* You will not stay in the wilderness indefinitely if you place your identity in Jesus as brother or sister and in the Father as Lord. There is life after the wilderness. The good news now is that we do not have to be idle. We can do something about our wilderness experience! The wilderness is a proving ground. It is a place of testing. Although we see the Jewish nation was tested and did not fare well in their wilderness walk, you do not have to follow their examples.

No other time or place in Jesus' life did Satan go on the offensive except on the cross. Humanity now can thank Jesus that we do not have to go to the cross. No other place in your life will Satan go on the attack, except in the wilderness, and only in the wilderness. Understand there is a purpose. There is Jesus. He has shown us a way through the wilderness. Take the examples He has given you, examples for purpose. Unbelief is not an option!

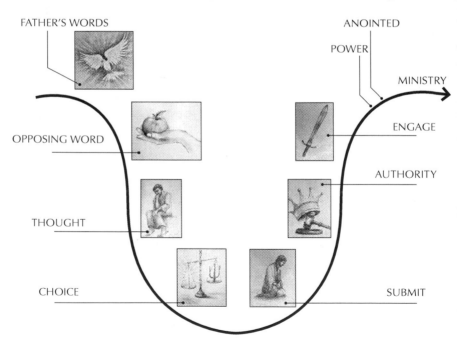

Jesus walked the road. We see the road map. It is a *Road Map through the Wilderness.*

CHAPTER 33

Validation?

I Corinthians 10:13(NKJV) declares, *"No temptation has overtaken you except such that is common to man; but God is faithful who will not allow you to be tempted beyond what you are able, but with temptation will also make the way of escape that you may be able to bear it."* Let us see Jesus in the wilderness and that He has given us a *Road Map Through the Wilderness,* a way out, a *"way of escape,"* an opportunity to release you from Satan's grip and all the pain and suffering he brings with that. It is not a given for you to stay in as Satan would have you think.

Hebrews 2:18(NKJV), *"For in that He Himself has suffered, being tempted, He is able to aid those who are tempted."* The Lord has now given us a detailed provision to get out. Could it be that *Road Map Through the Wilderness* is that aid, or at the very least, an aid?

Isaiah 43:18-19(NKJV), *"Do not remember the former things, nor consider the things of old. Behold, I will do a new thing, now it shall spring forth; shall you not know it? I will even make a road in the wilderness and rivers in the desert."* Throughout my life from my early thirties, the Lord has unfolded the words in this book. It, however, was not until recent years that

He led me to these scriptures above. By the messages in this book, the Lord unfolds a new understanding, new opportunity, if not a new direction for the church. I suppose time will tell us if *Road Map Through the Wilderness* is a reference in these scriptures mentioned above.

Consider, however, without exception, everyone completing this teaching has been enthusiastic about the message and has been ministered to in hearing it. It is the norm to receive testimony that it is changing lives. I have not only witnessed it here in the United States but from pastors in India who have sat through this message, literally on the other side of the world.

Enthusiastic responses appear to be a testimony to the validity of these words and their necessity. Is there a subtle, focused, aggressive attack by darkness on Christ's church around the world, focused on destroying those who are the biggest threat to our enemy, Satan? If so, it is most definitely a sign of the times.

The following questions, however, reflect what is most important about *Road Map Through the Wilderness.*

1. How can all this be brought together to a significance in the kingdom of God today?
2. How specifically can He bring power and anointing ultimately for any of us to be sent?
3. What is the key enabling all you have read here to be authentic in your life?
4. What is the catalyst for ministry to overflow in atomic proportions in your life?

The answer to each of these is to ask. Invite the Lord into your life. Make him Lord of your life, and simply ask. Will it unfold precisely when you think it should? It never has for me.

Will it unfold exactly how you think it should? It never has for me. **Isaiah 55:8(NKJV)**, *"For My thoughts are not your thoughts,* *nor are your ways my ways, says the Lord.*" Our Lord's thoughts are so much greater than ours. He can and will move in mighty ways that we cannot comprehend.

Following is a testimony that illustrates this very point.

It is now 11:59 p.m. on October 30, 2019, the eve of Halloween. It was not my intention to write at this time, but I was awakened, impressed to do so. I suppose there is a reason for the timing, but I am not aware of that now.

Several hours ago, just before a *Road Map Through the Wilderness* class, an attendee shared the following with me. She said she previously attended a church that did not preach or teach much of the Word of God. There was little depth in the messages, and she described her previous thoughts of the Lord as a fairy tale. Her only belief in Jesus was that He was a person. She is now attending a church that preaches and lives the Word.

Before attending classes, she had not understood nor heard any of the concepts in *Road Map Through the Wilderness*. Righteous anger, spiritually taking authority, speaking the Word at dark personalities, and other concepts shared were not familiar to her.

This night, in the ninth week of the ten-week series, she shared that she has been having terrible nightmares recently. She said that one dream was so horrible that she feels she has seen literal hell. Currently being in the workplace, these dreams were affecting her sleep, which negatively affected her performance at work. In one of her dreams, not consciously, she implemented one of the Road Map truths. She simply said, "No," to the darkness that was creating her dreams. Her report, as a result of this resistance, is that the nightmares were gone immediately. Spiritual oppression ceased. She is now sleeping well through the night. Even in her subconscious, in her dream, the implementation of Road Map truths was authentically effective in the conscious, a demonstration of real power. By this testimony and others, the messages in *Road*

Map Through the Wilderness appear to be valid in supplying real needs in the lives of individuals today.

Father, I thank you for giving us the privilege of hearing your voice, explaining to us how to get out of the wilderness, and what to do when we get out! I thank you that you have a plan for us just as you had a plan for Jesus coming out of the wilderness with your power. Please help us to understand that truth in our most profound wilderness experiences. Thank you for giving us hope, focus, direction, and strength to move up and out.

In the name of the one who gave all that we might receive all. His name is Jesus. Amen!

Epilogue

Many years ago, I asked the Lord repeatedly, "Lord, may I hear your voice?" The irony is that in my prayer, I asked for something quite different from hearing a theme so detailed as this book. I was looking for Him to validate His presence in my life. By His grace, He did that and also shared this message that I pass on to you. **John 15:7(NKJV)** says, *"If you abide in Me and my words abide in you, you will ask what you desire, and it shall be done for you."* He has done that and so much more.

In less than twenty-four hours after completing the final chapter of this book, this fantastic event occurred to place God's thumbprint on His message of grace. My wife, Donna, and I have devotions every morning using *My Wisdom Notes* by Dr. Mike Murdock. I opened the email received that very morning with these perfectly timed words on the screen in front of me. "Expect the supernatural in your life." Supernaturally, now I have received what I have yearned to hear for more than three decades. By God's grace, however, this message is given, not from any merit of man. By God's grace only, I can share it with you. The *"vail of the temple was torn,"* We can sit at His feet in the throne room. Praise the Lord! It is my prayer that you receive *Road Map Through the Wilderness* unto power, anointing, all to be sent. And that you determine by His grace, he has freely given it to you.

Postlude
My Wilderness Experience

I had the privilege to walk through several wilderness experiences. All three were obvious attacks from darkness, designed to harm people I love and claim dominion in their lives. All attacks have caused considerable struggle and stress that has impacted my life and theirs. These have motivated me to dig deeper into His Word, seek His Spirit, and see His mighty hand work in otherwise hopeless scenarios. Here is one of my wilderness experiences.

My immediate family spent a Thanksgiving meal at noon in 1977 with my parents on our farm. Later that evening, while celebrating Thanksgiving with my wife's parents, I received a phone call from my mother saying my father had just passed from a heart attack, only hours after we had left. We rushed back home. I was ushered immediately upon arrival into the living room. My mother shared details about my father's life that were foreign to me. A lengthy discussion, lasting several hours unfolded a World War II saga which indicated that my father had been the leader in a secret group. They were assigned to seek out and eliminate Nazi spies operating in a specific geographic region in the United States. Her desire was for me to see my father as a hero. He had not wanted me to know, feeling that the actions necessary for these activities would offend or otherwise negatively affect how

I felt about him. My mother explained situations and scenarios in considerable detail. The stories continued for hours. Remarkably, these unusual stories seemed to be confirmed in my mind as I remembered observances and events over my lifetime as a child. As my mother shared with conviction, she convinced me that her information was credible and trustworthy. Looking back, I believe those stories had some merit. I suspect, however, a power that was not of God distorted her stories to the point that makes most all her words difficult to understand with any substance of truth. Unfortunately, this event was the beginning of an extended twenty-five year ordeal of dealing with my mother's disease.

As an only child, my father, my mother, and I appeared to be, and in my judgment were, an ideal family. In my high school senior class yearbook, I named my parents "My Most Valuable Possession." We were quite close. My pain, therefore, was deep and prolonged by events I will share with you. These events were difficult enough to experience but going through all as an only child was so severe, especially when I saw the breakdown of what I had thought was an ideal childhood. It took a considerable toll on me. There are too many events to discuss here, but suffice it to say, it was difficult to manage, living two hundred thirty miles away from my mother.

After my father died at age fifty-two and living so far away, I could not observe much of my mother's behavior except that she became distant as she shared more bizarre ongoing stories. Emotional phone calls came from family and friends close to her, who were concerned about her behavior. She was becoming a total recluse. Eventually, she alienated everyone from her life, including me. One day while visiting her, it happened. She said I was not to see her anymore. She, "needed her space."

The calls from family and friends continued. "Your mother is now wearing a revolver strapped to her side," one said. I finally decided to intervene. I went to visit the county mental health office in her area. The local mental health department could not assist me. They said that an individual had to observe an act of behavior where my mother demonstrated a threat of bodily harm to herself or others and report the occurrence within three days. I was living hundreds of miles away and received reports from individuals that were close to her. I just could not convince them to call the mental health department. Nobody back home would "get involved." Unfortunately, the mental health department did not consider my reports valid because I was not a direct observer and therefore had no credibility in the law's eyes.

Finally, Mother stepped over the line. Her first arrest for threatening a neighbor with a pistol landed her in a mental facility. The police found several guns in her home. I learned later that officials admitted her with a diagnosis of paranoid schizophrenia. Her first admittance lasted six months and then later for a year.

I was able to determine that she thought I was trying to sneak into her bedroom and poison her bedsheets to kill her. I learned a night watchman she hired was encouraging her by training her to use a pistol. He introduced her to an attorney in a large metropolitan city who wrote me out of her will. Also, she hired a private investigator to investigate me. One night at about 3 a.m., I received the call. I said, "Hello." She screamed, "Don, this is your mother. I want you to know; I curse the day you were born. You will never know when or where but know this. I WILL KILL YOU!" She then hung up.

The second arrest occurred in a large city one hundred fifty miles away from home when she was in front of a convenience store out of state. The police found a gun in the car and charged her for carrying a weapon without a permit. Jail time was thirty days while awaiting her trial. While there, inmates raped her. OH, MY LORD, WHERE ART THOU?!!!!!! I was not allowed to see her, as she would not permit me due to the delusions she had about me. She was committed to the same mental home and became a patient for one year.

Although much heartache occurred in this twenty-five plus year saga, there were many victories also in this walk. One night I was praying at my altar at home, the woodpile behind my house. As I was weeping that night, I heard that still soft voice, not audibly, yet saying the name of an individual from back home. I will call him JD. The name kept getting stronger in my mind, JD, JD. He was a family friend who I had known on a first-name basis for most of my life. I needed to travel back home for some personal business. Before departing, I called JD and asked if I could speak to him. He invited me to come to his house one evening. My pastor was supportive through this long ordeal, and I invited him to go with me back home for the trip.

JD invited us into his kitchen when we approached the door. I asked him if he was aware of my mother's behavior in the community, and he acknowledged. I then asked if he had any information about her. He said, "No, I did not have any contact with her except for that time last fall, and ..." I did not catch the reference of the incident, but my pastor quickly placed his hand on JD's forearm and said, "Tell us about last fall."

JD started to unfold an experience at his house. One night my mother arrived on his doorstep, frantic. She indicated that she had been racing down a secondary road, "running away" from the FBI, Nazis, or some other adversary that I cannot recall, and arrived on his porch wanting to come in. She spent an extended amount of time there, sharing with him what was going on in her life or what she perceived to be true. For me, it was the "mother lode" of information. She told him about her then-current scenario, as she understood it. Names, locations, and other details regarding her life were shared. I now had a wealth of credible information that shed light on the darkness she walked in for years. I now had information provided that, when researched, enabled me to discover facts about her well-being or lack thereof. The Lord had orchestrated this whole scenario. He miraculously led me to JD, who helped me move on to the next step of her ultimate healing.

Another intervention unfolded years later. My mother was then in the state mental hospital. In another instance of being led, the Lord maneuvered me into her presence at the hospital. "Patient rights" prevented me from seeing her, as she would not agree to the visit from me. The Lord miraculously opened a door that enabled me to walk into the hospital and have a dialogue with her. While praying in my office, I felt strongly to call the hospital and tell them I was an only child, that I have not seen her for years, and to insist on seeing her, and that I did not have to be too pleasant about it!" This approach is amazing, as my temperament has always been rather mild. This activity eventually evolved to periodic visits and a slow reconnection with my mother that led to the next scene.

With our relationship somewhat established, the professional staff at the hospital gave her leave to accompany me on day trips. With the farm sold, we would drive slowly by the fields and buildings to reminisce, go to dinner, and enjoy a nice leisurely drive back. That and other excursions helped to strengthen our worn and torn relationship. Without exception, before I drove to meet with her, the Lord would instruct me to do something that would contribute to her healing. On one occasion, He told me to say something specific to her. I had no understanding of its significance to her mental state, nor do I now recall what it was. I do remember it was something that I should say in a quiet setting. There was no opportunity all day. Late in the afternoon, we arrived at her favorite restaurant. I turned off the car and saw the opportunity to speak just what I heard. Immediately she placed her hands in her face and wept. This statement opened up a guarded area of her mind that allowed me to talk in detail about issues in her life. After decades, I was now able to speak to my mother. This powerful moment in our relationship assisted in her ultimate healing.

One day, as I left the mental hospital building; a staff member followed me outside, asking me to stop. As I turned around, he introduced himself and indicated he was a caseworker assigned to help my mother. Then he said these words. "Mr. Claycomb, I have been in the mental health profession for 17 years. In my whole career, I have never seen anybody rooted in their delusions as deeply as your mother. Frankly, we cannot do anything with her. However, every time you come to visit her, we see improvement. We do not know what you are doing, but keep it up." I took the opportunity to share how it was the Lord's intervention in her life. I hoped others heard the same story as he went back into the building.

"The rest of the story" is this: My mother was released from the hospital with ongoing care from the local county mental health clinic. Ironically, the same person that initially told me they could not help me became her caseworker. By involving me in my mother's treatment, our relationship grew strong. In 2005, my mother moved two hundred thirty miles away from her lifelong community to our town and lived only one mile away from our house. She needed her medication regularly as there was a chemical imbalance in her brain. However, in the last several years of her life, the Lord gave us a total restoration of our relationship and an even greater bond than we ever had before. He restored her sanity and ultimate freedom from torment. She passed on to be with my father and the Lord in July of 2008. As for the stories about my father, I feel most are rooted in truth. Unfortunately, the distortion of mental disease blurs them to the point of little clarity about which I hope to ask Jesus when I go on home.

This, one of my wilderness experiences, tested me far more than I ever thought I could endure. However, He did provide a depth of knowledge and understanding about wilderness experiences as He led me through them. The Lord has laid a message on my heart now, possibly to share in the church community. The message's primary focus is on Jesus' walk down the road of His wilderness experiences. Hmmm!

Words cannot express the emotional pain I endured or demonstrate the fear that welled within me for years. Words cannot shed a glimpse of the helplessness and hopelessness I experienced. Months turned into years. Years became decades. Thank God for an understanding and supportive wife who walked this same path with me. Thank God for power, love, and anointing in healing my mother from her torment and restoring our relationship. I had the privilege of ushering her on to our Lord's arms as she took her last breath. Our God is truly amazing. This scenario was one of my wilderness experiences.

Printed in the United States
By Bookmasters